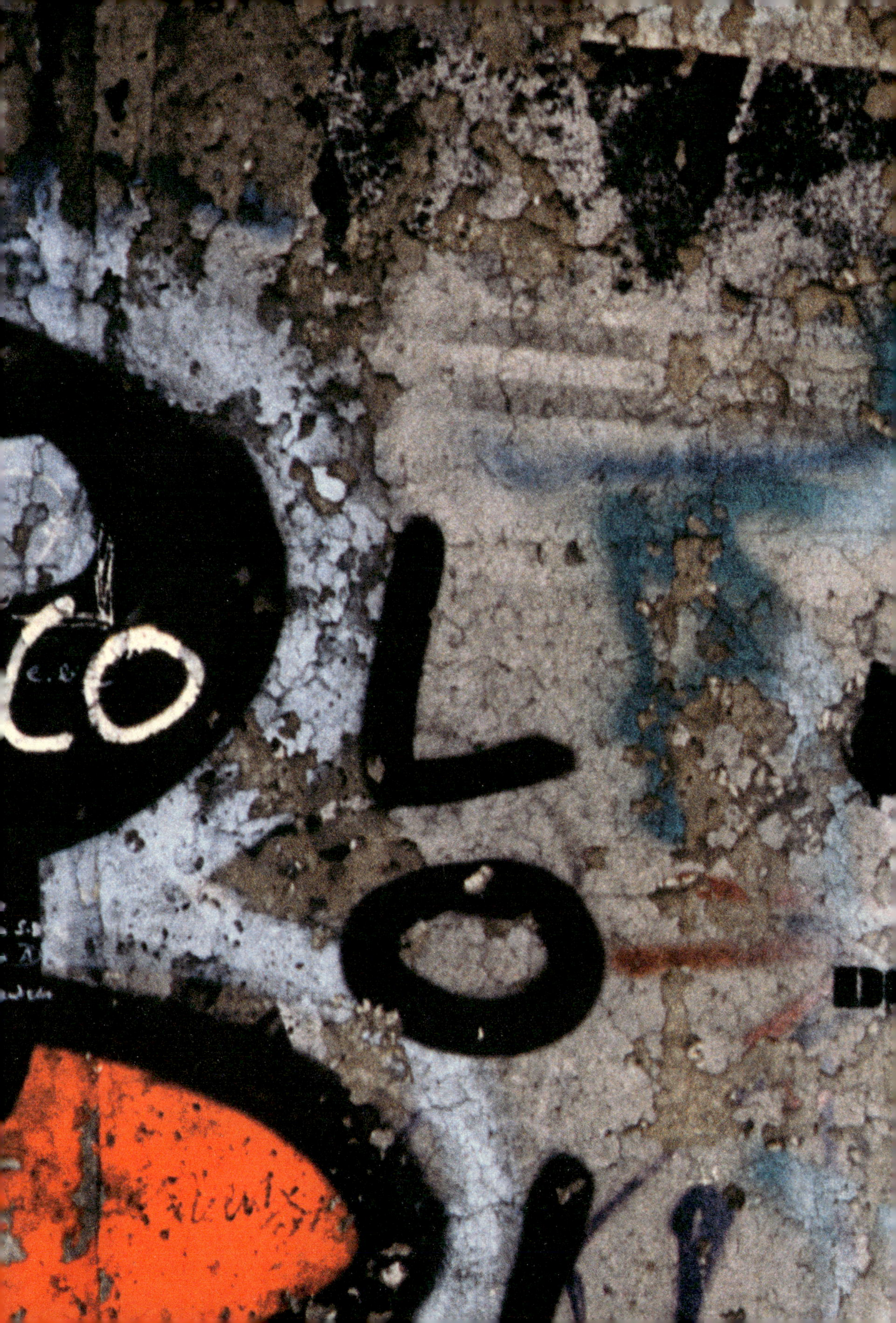

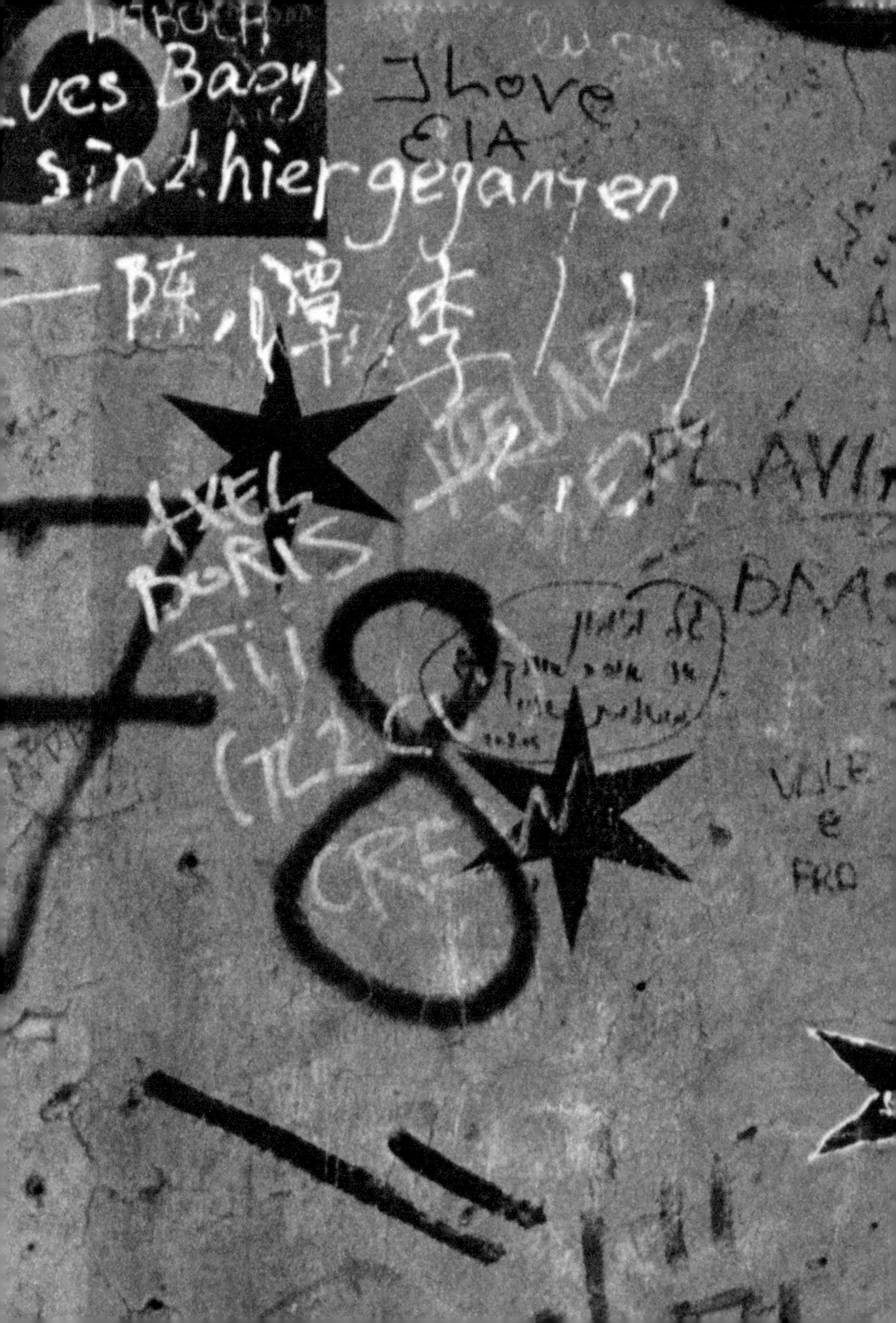

ves Baoys I Love
EIA
sind hier gegangen

Axel
Boris

PLAY

BM

VALE
e
FRD

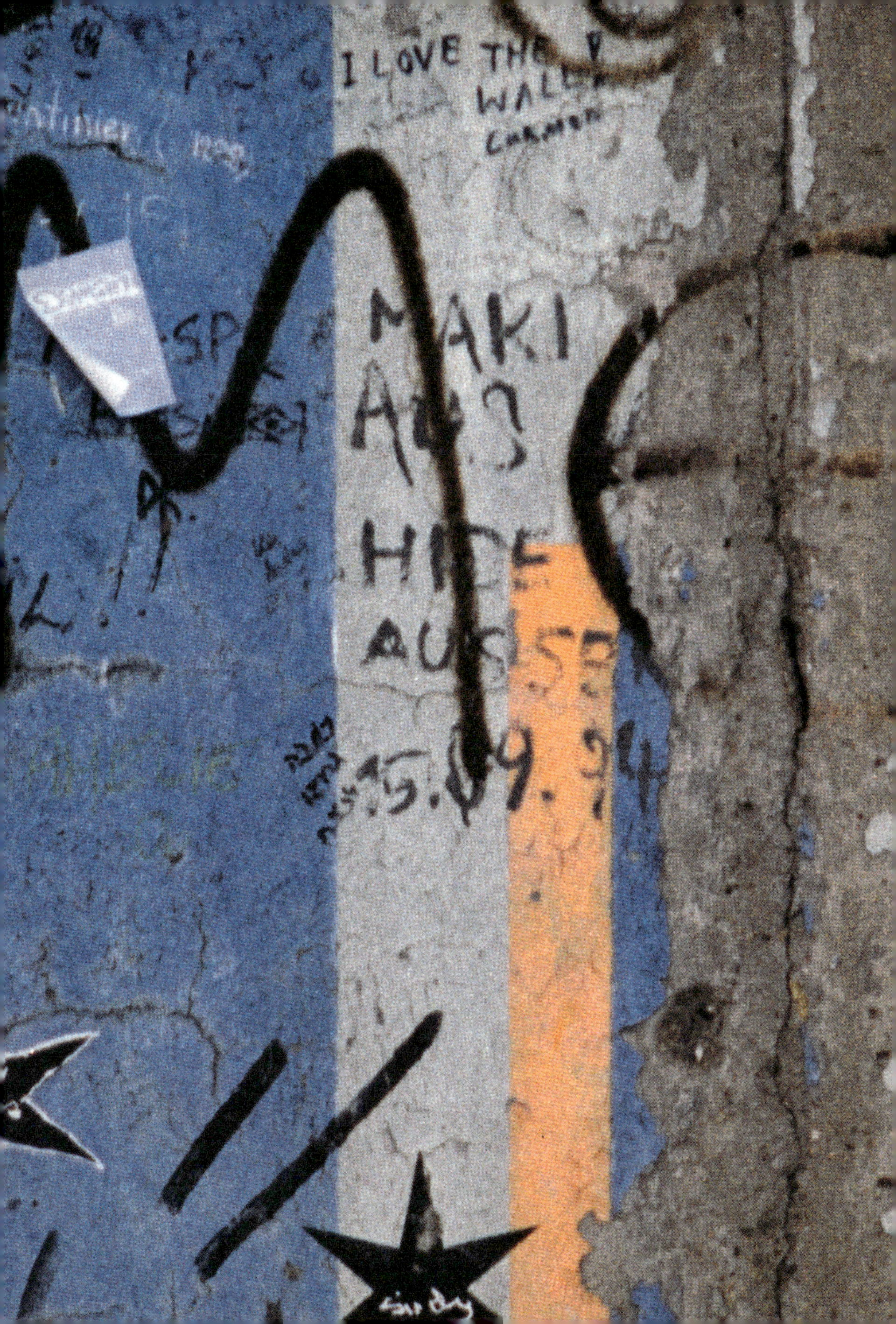
I LOVE THE WALL
CARMEN
MAKI
HIDE
15.09.94

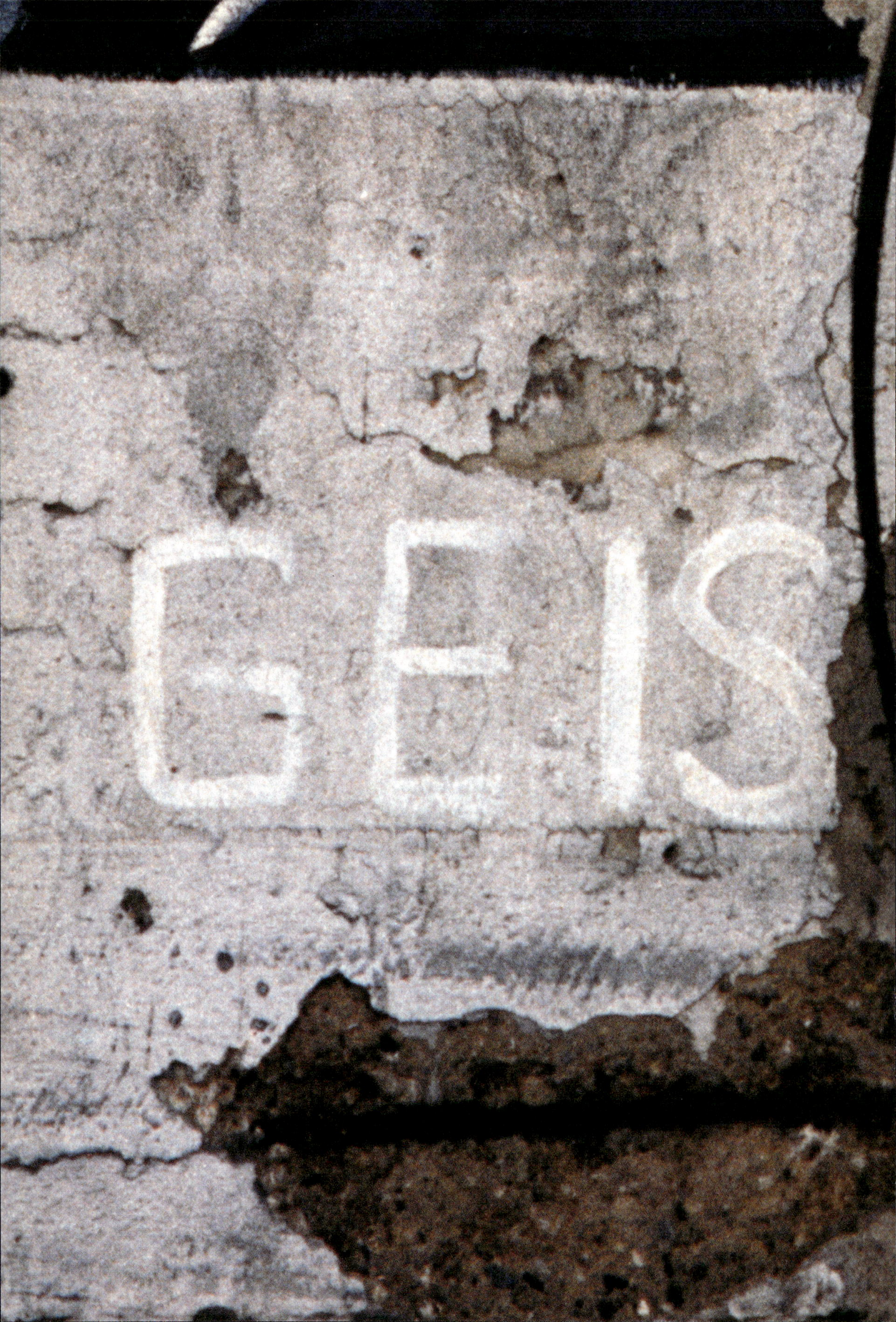
GEIS

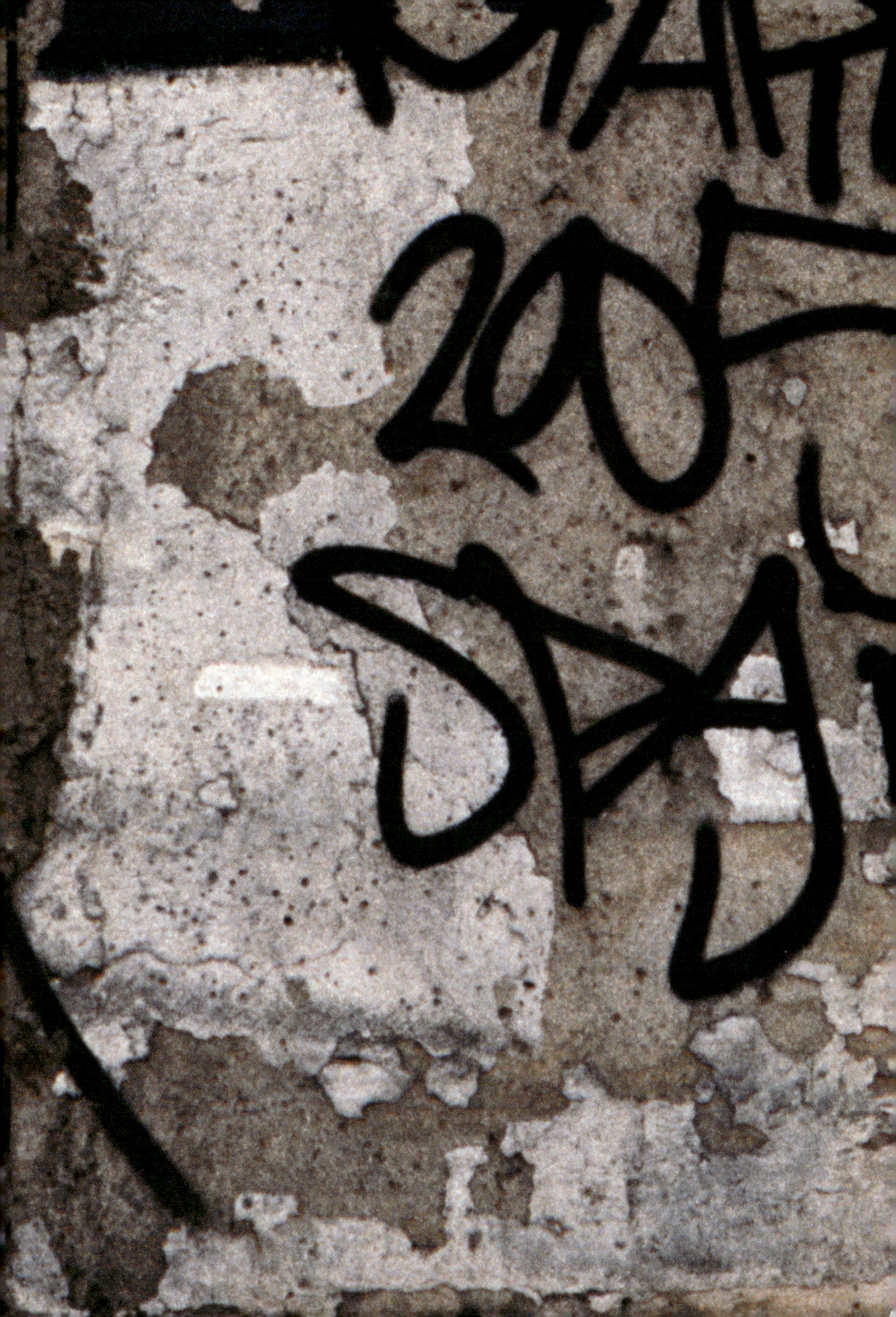

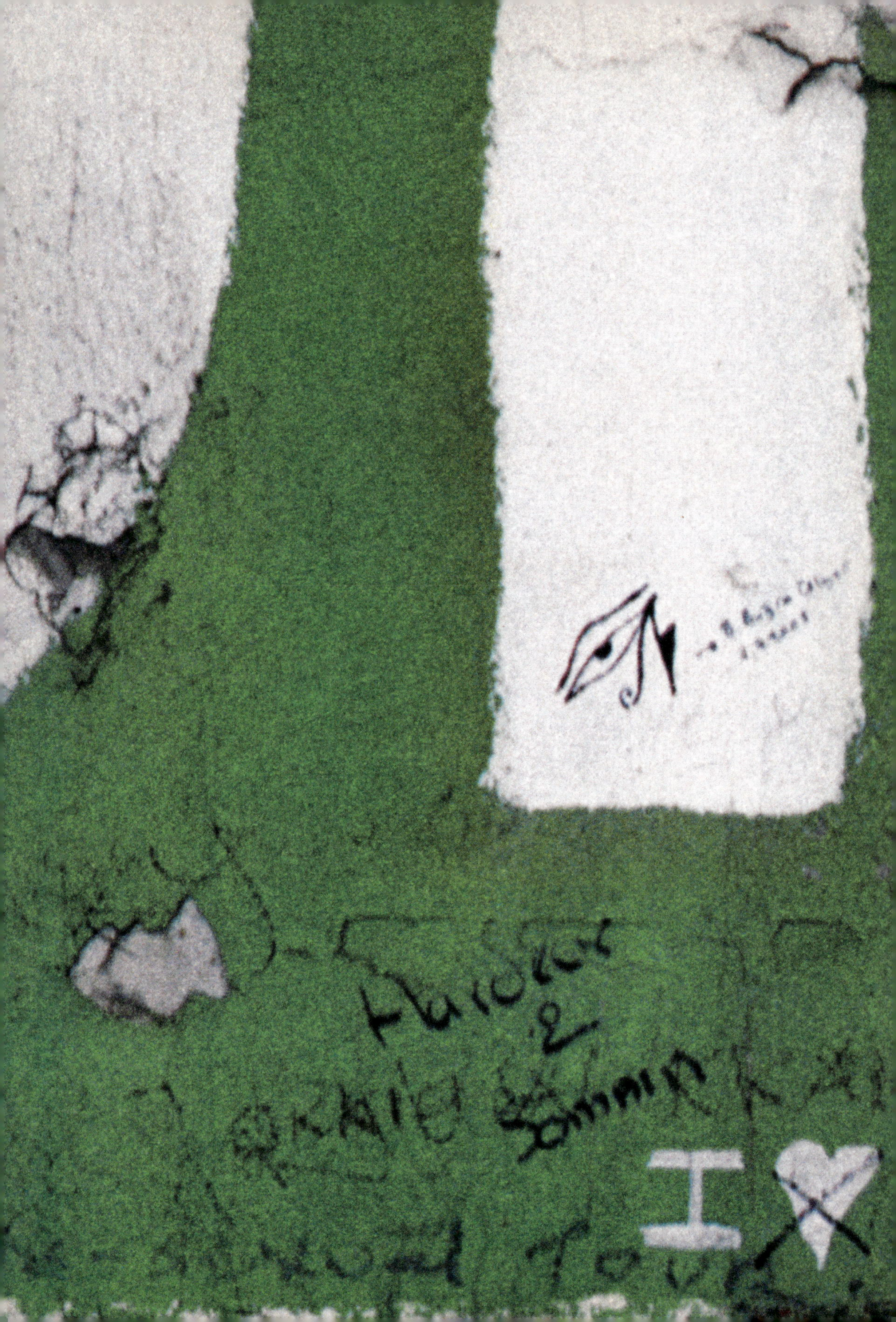

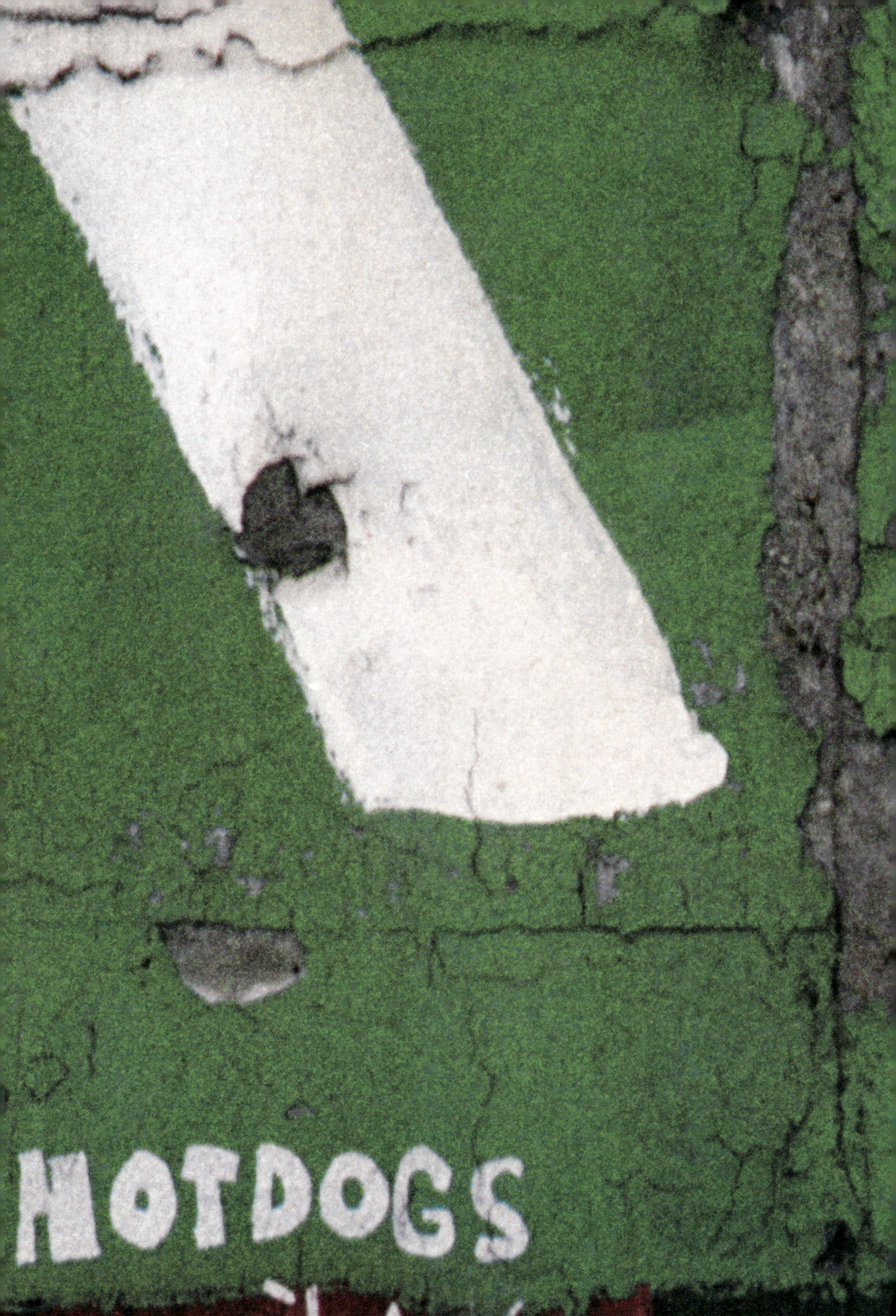
HOTDOGS

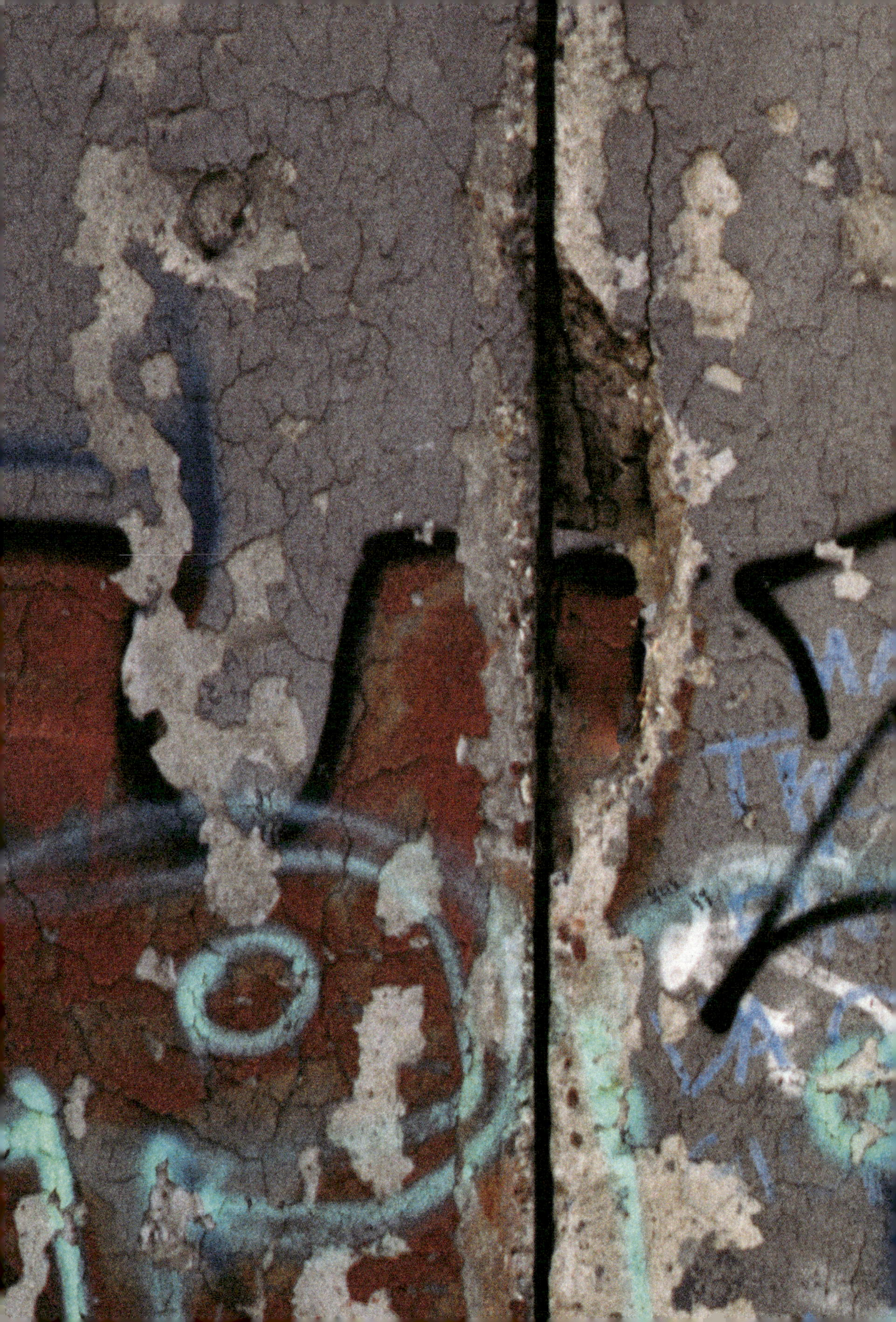

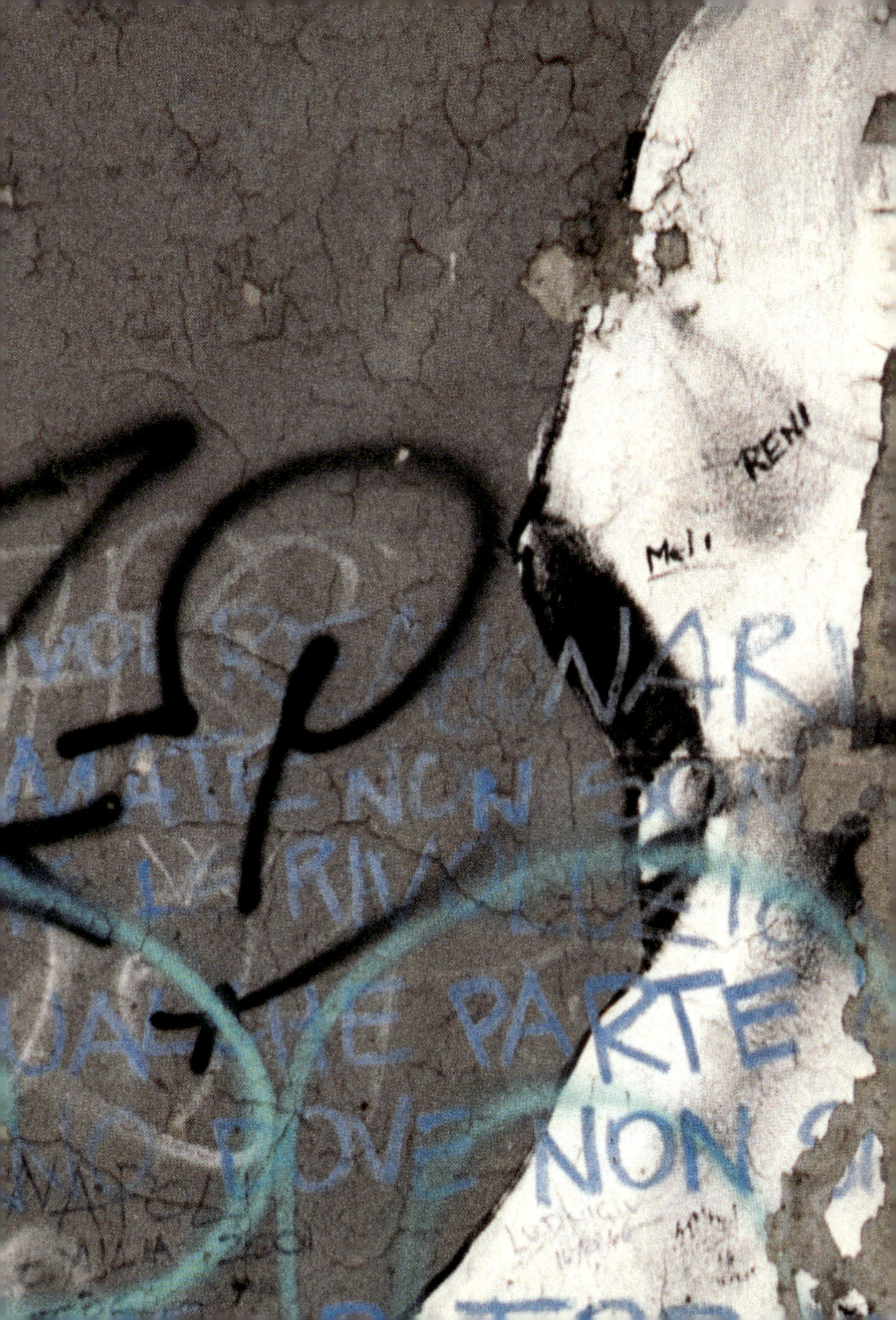

RENI
Meli
VOI S
PIÙ ONAR
MATE NON SO
LY RIV
PARTE
NON
DOVE

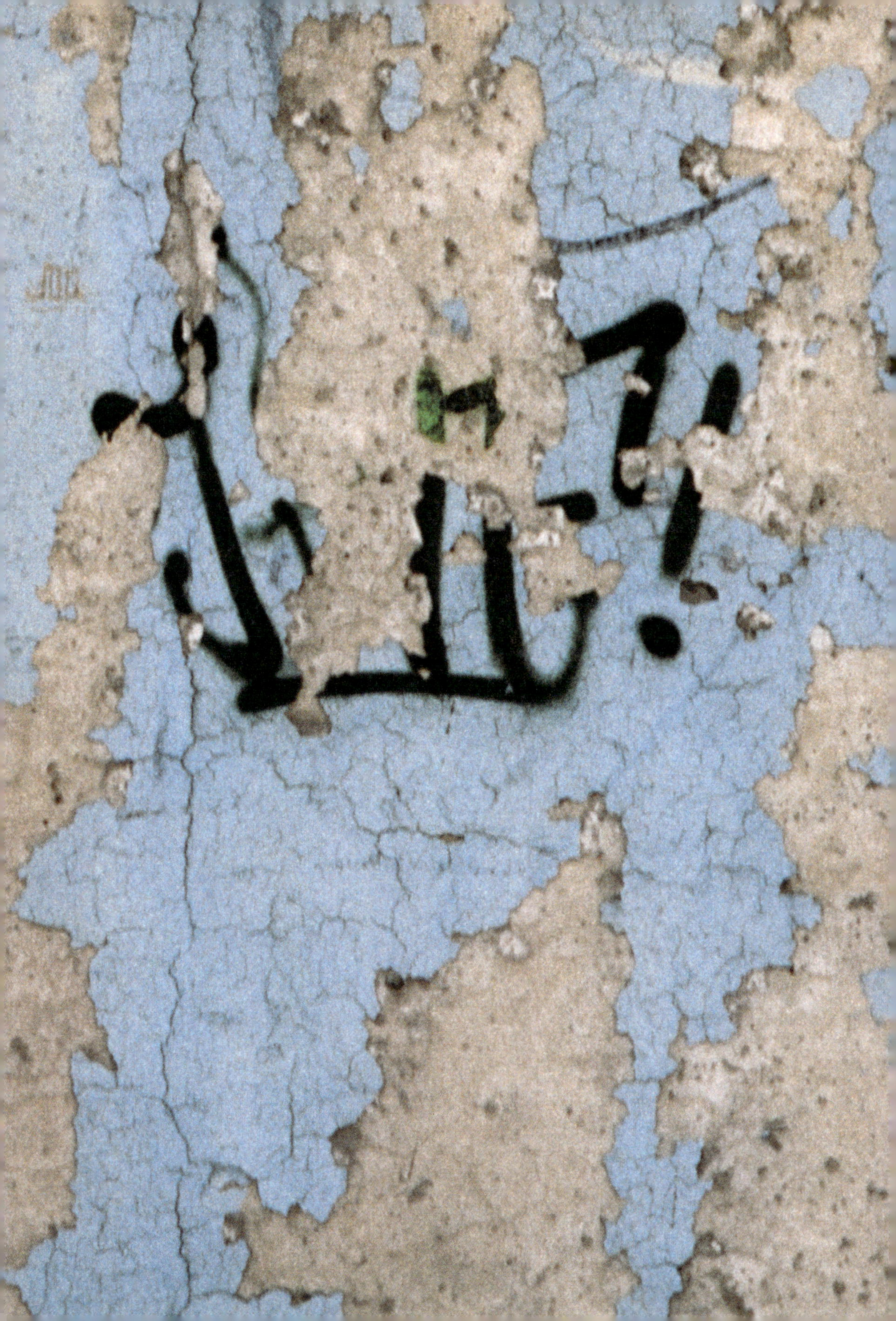

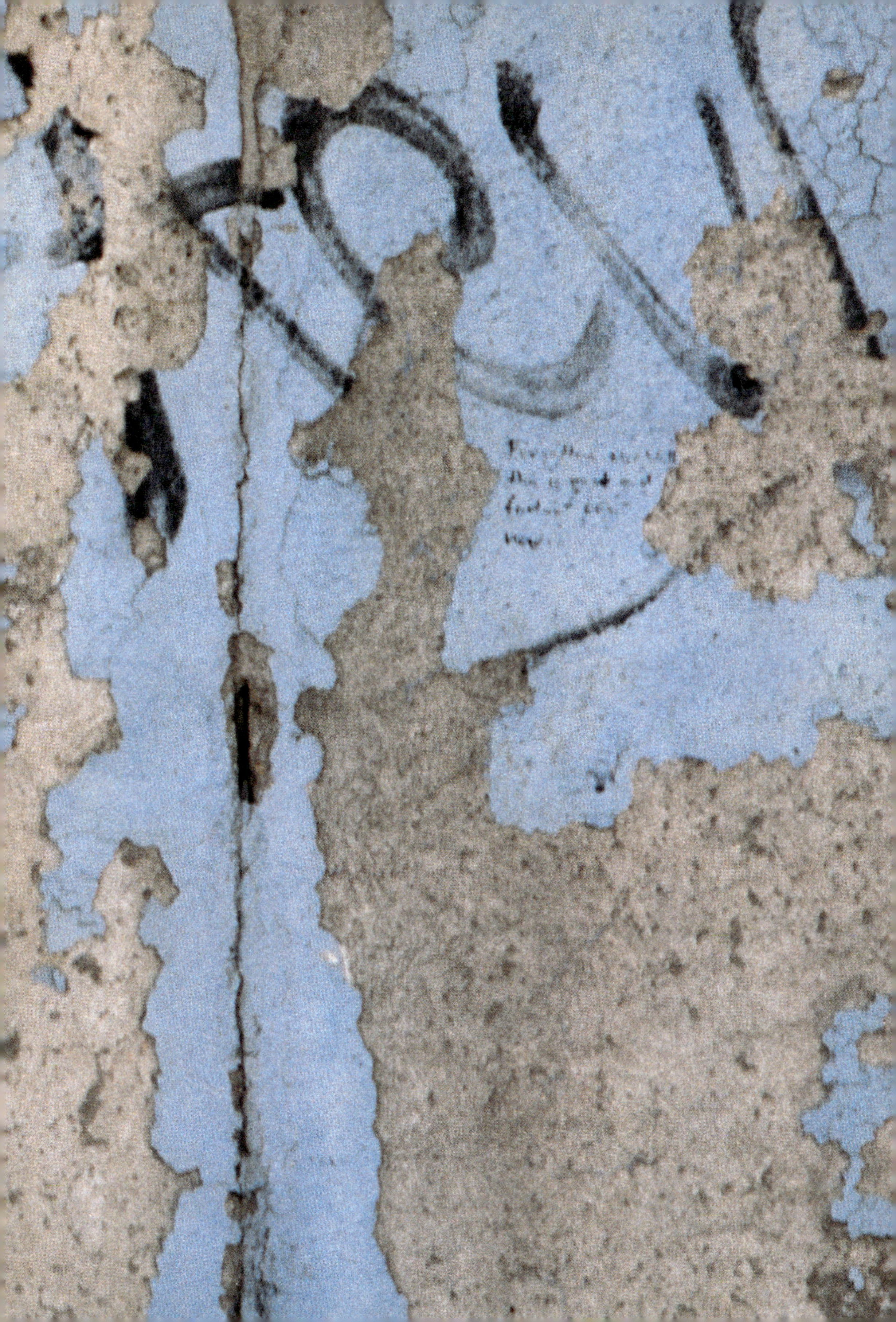

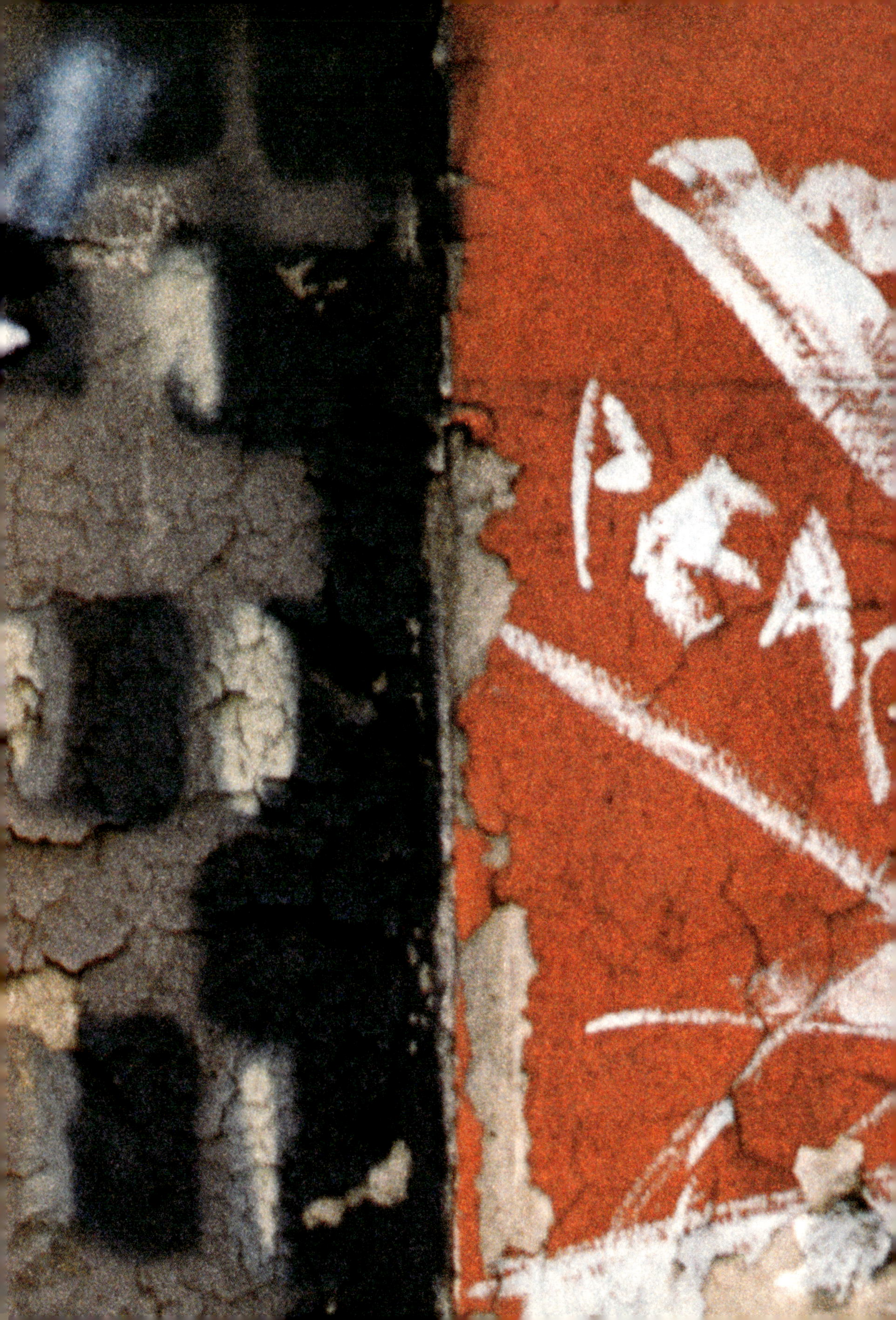

PEA

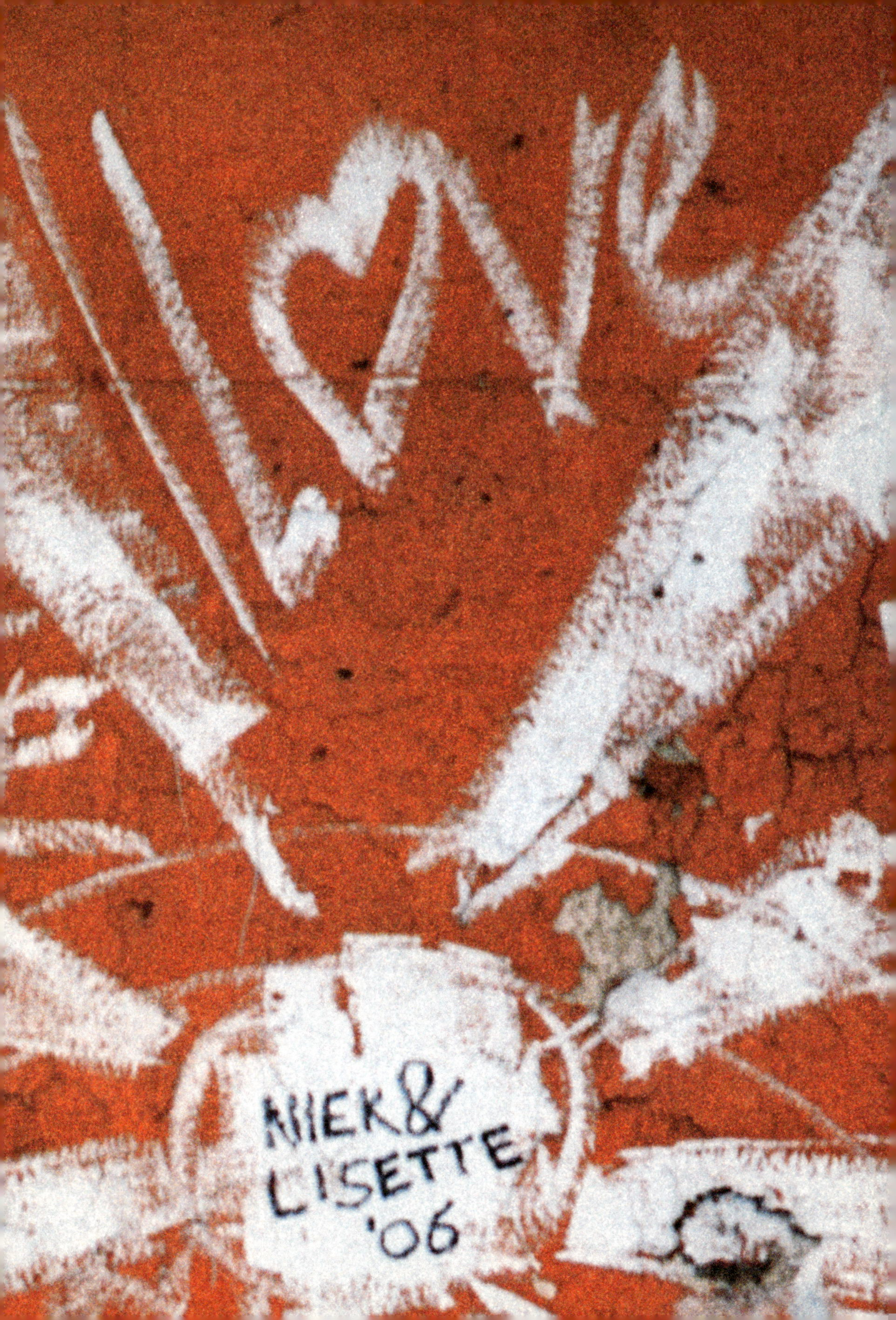
NIEK &
LISETTE
'06

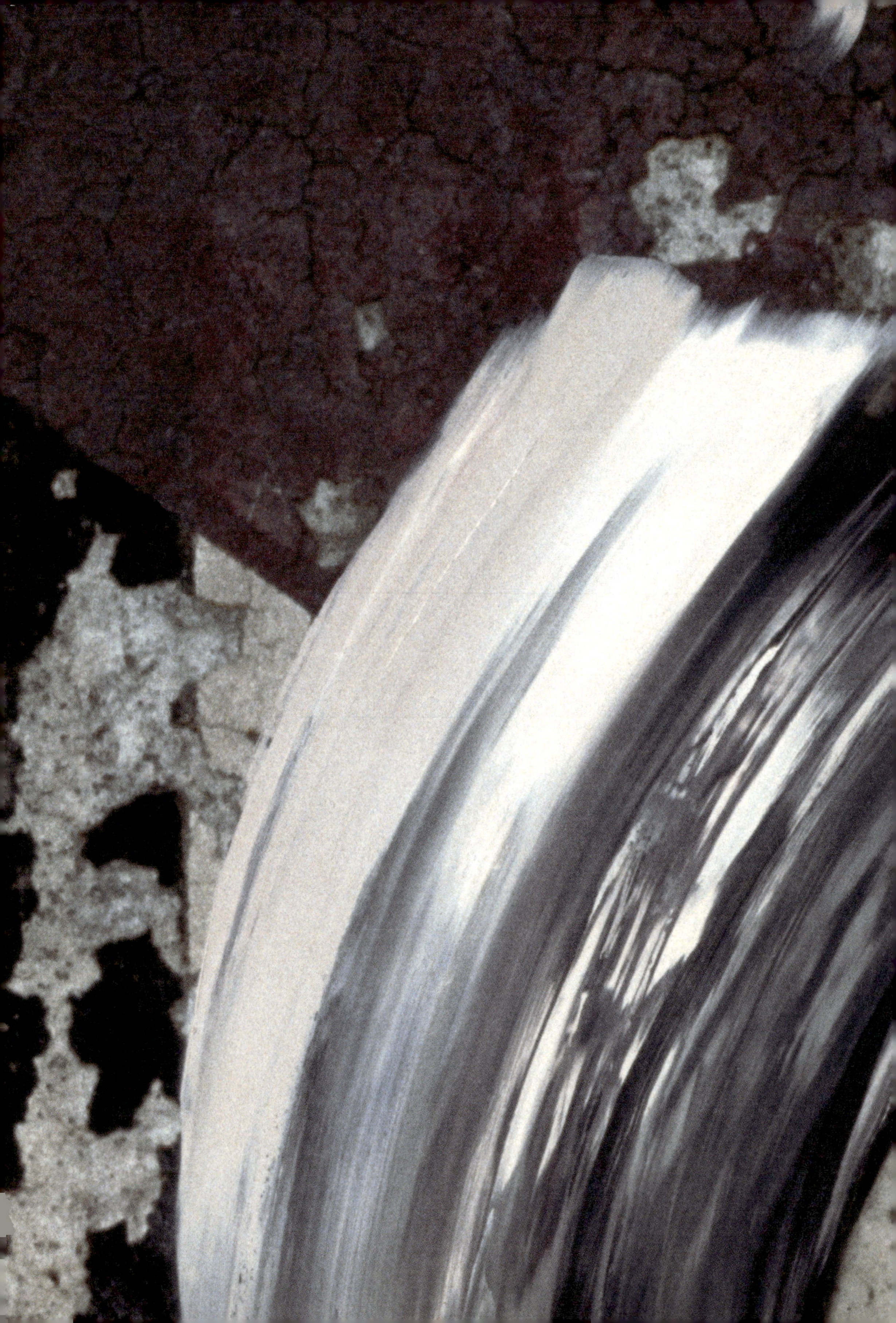

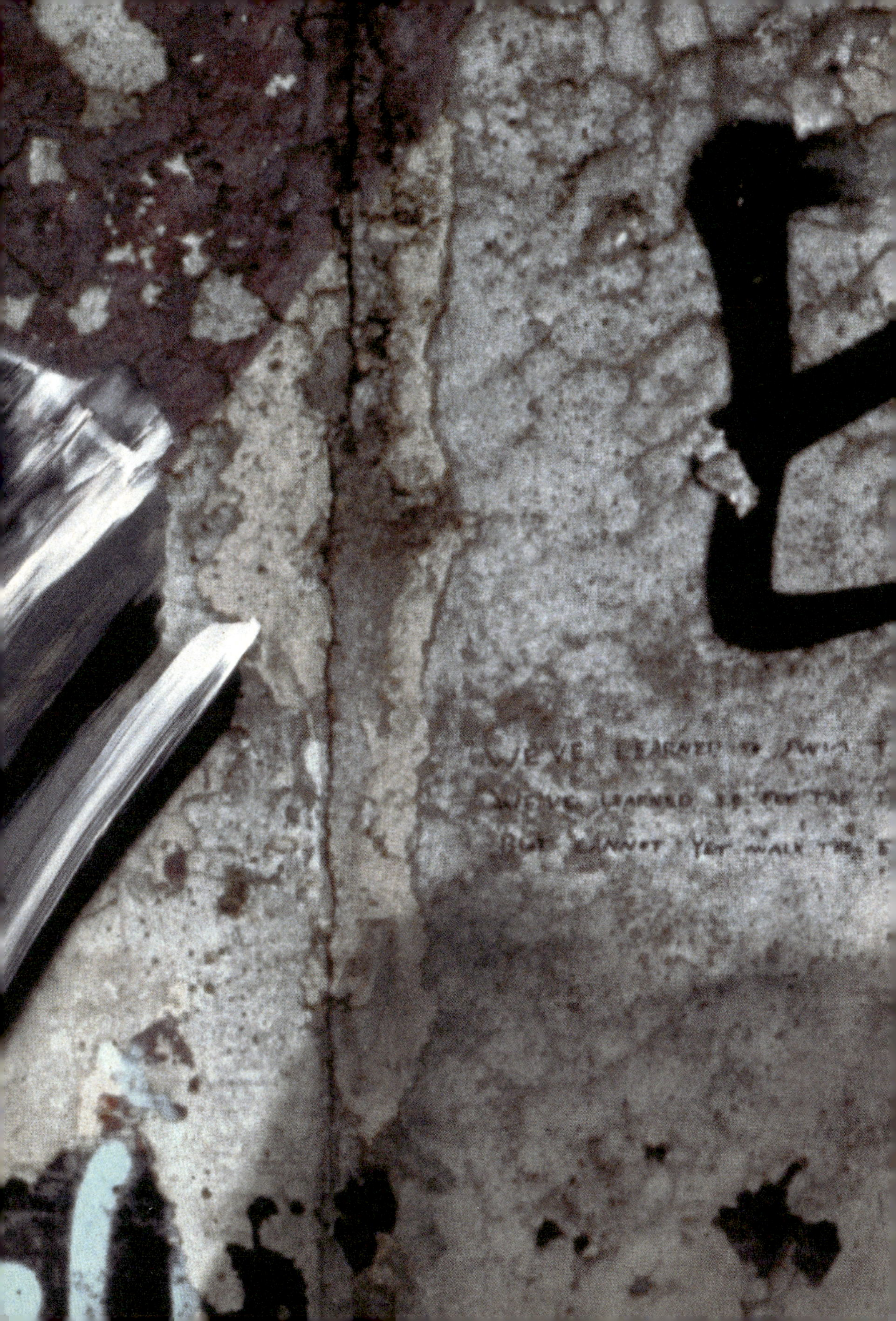
WE'VE LEARNED TO FLY
WE'VE LEARNED TO PER
BUT CANNOT YET WALK THE E

Marc Lüders

East Side Gallery

KERBER ART

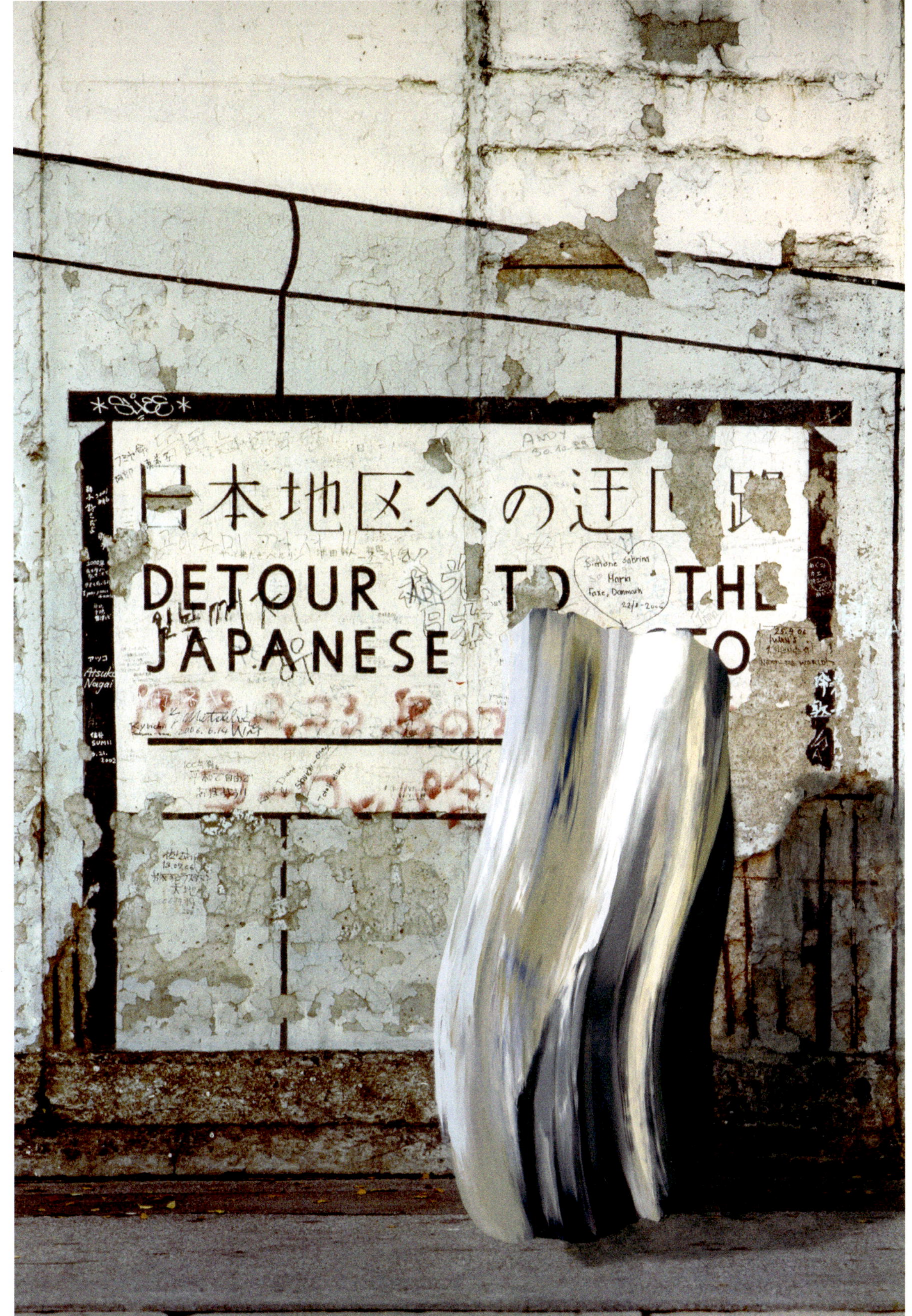
日本地区への迂回路
DETOUR TO THE
JAPANESE

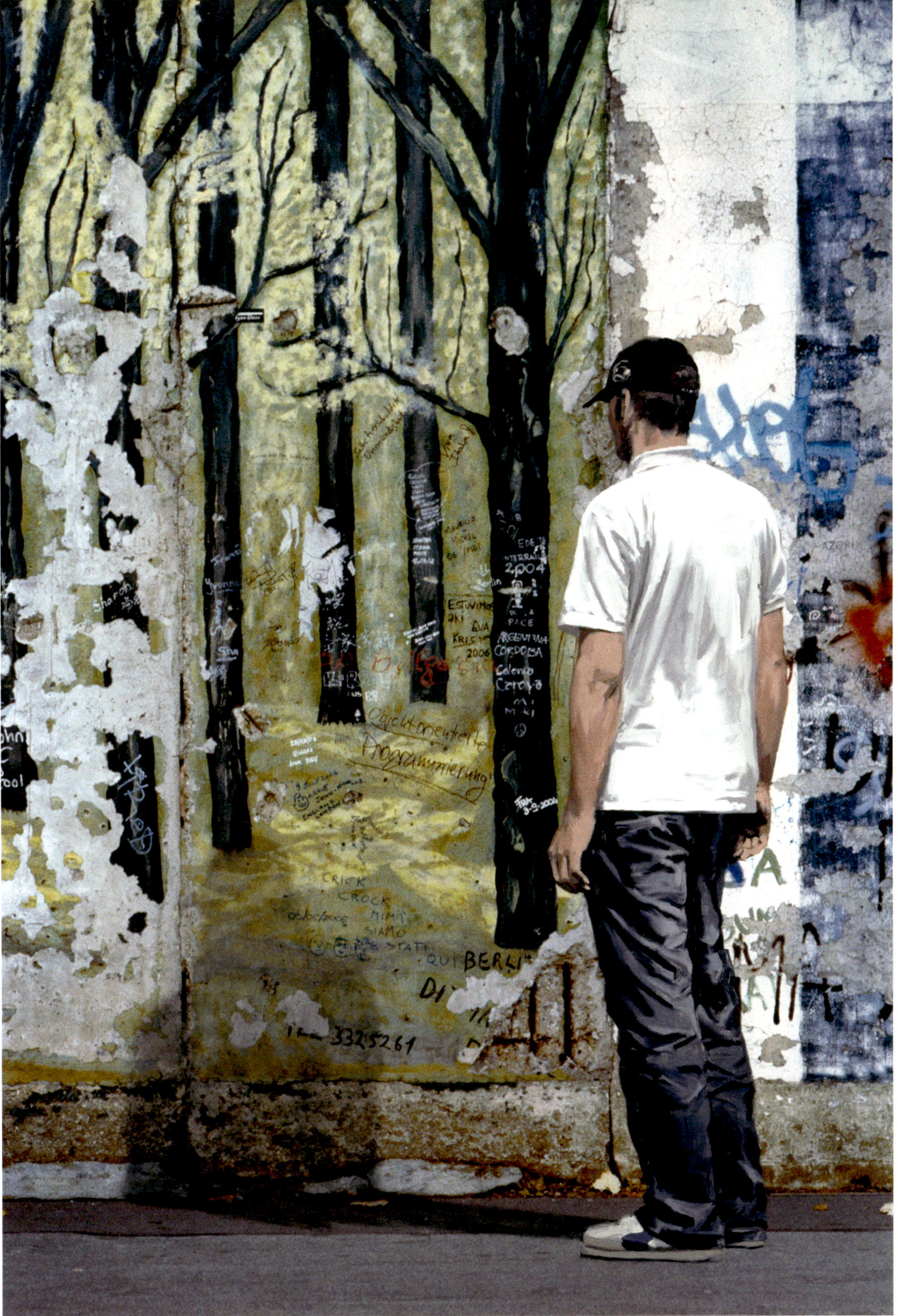

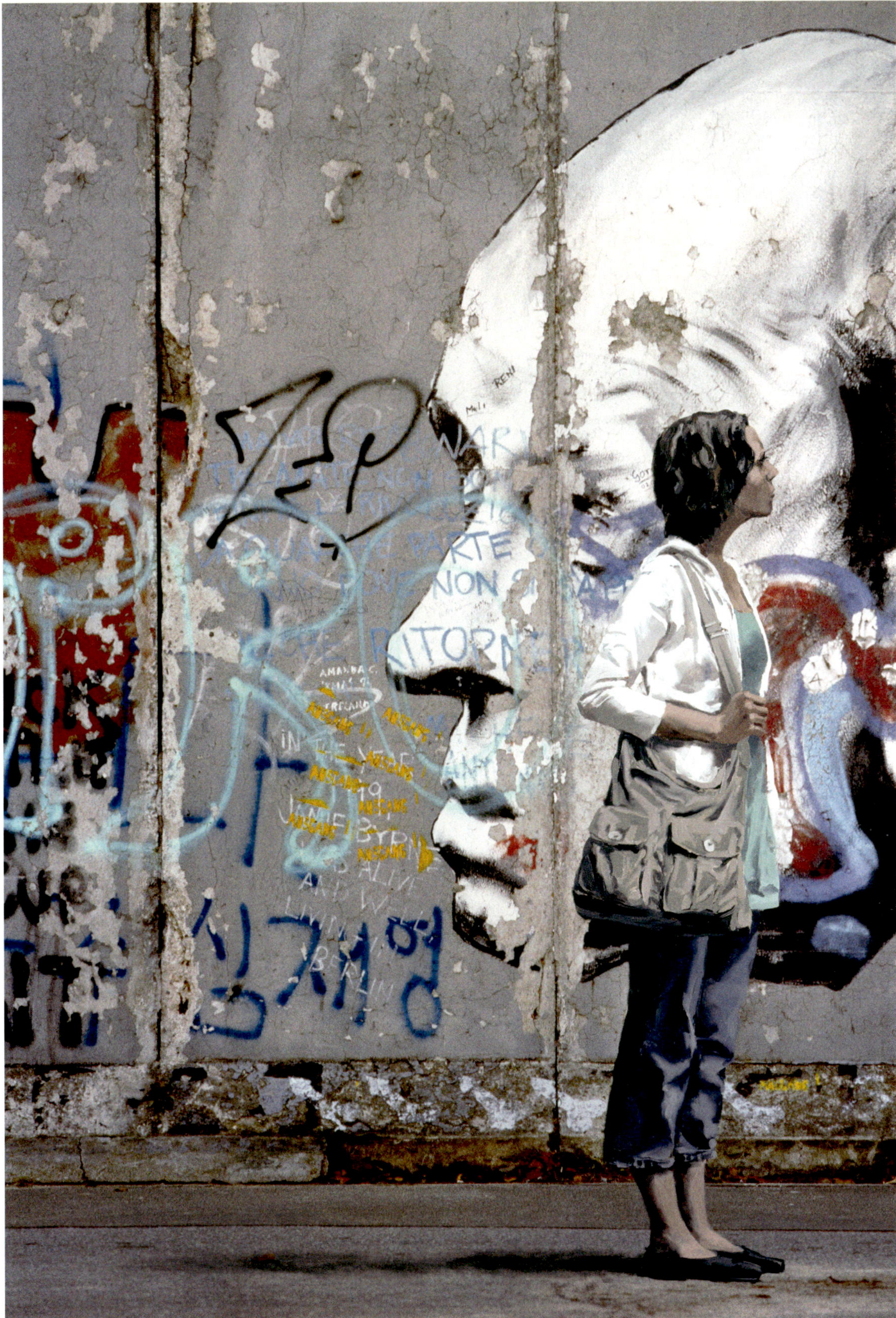

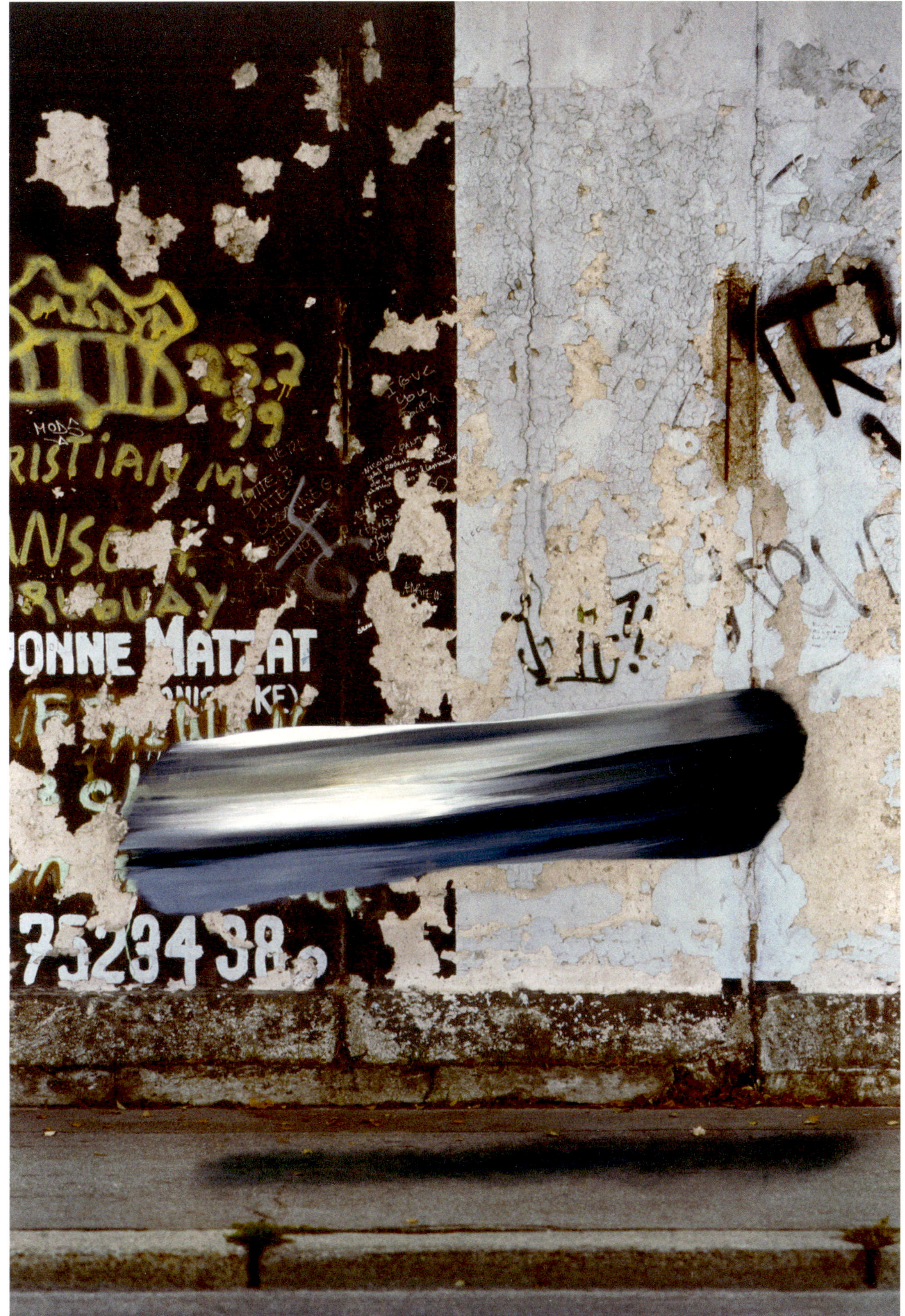
MODS
RISTIAN M.
ANSO
RUGUAY
JONNE MATZAT
75234 38.

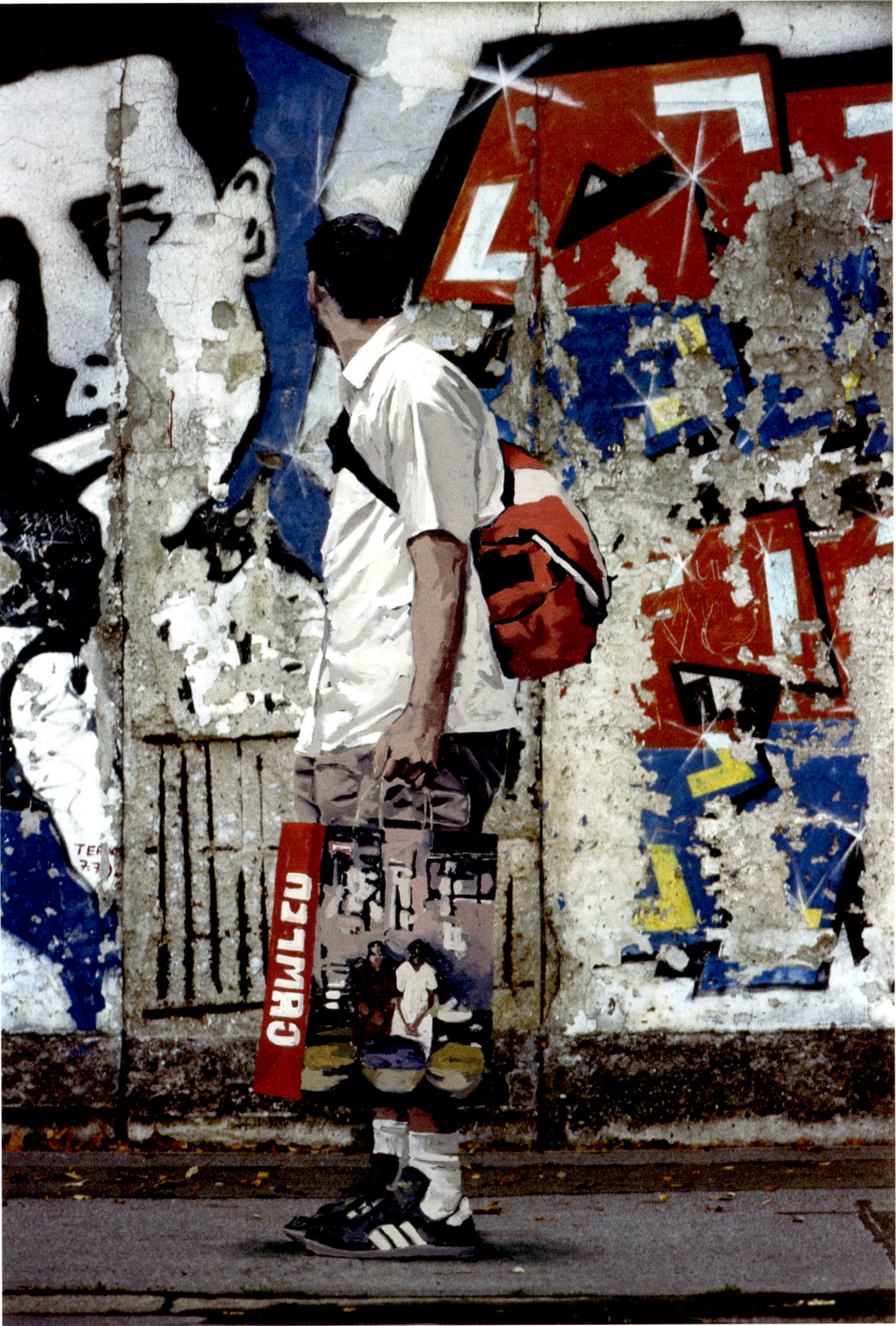
CAMILLO

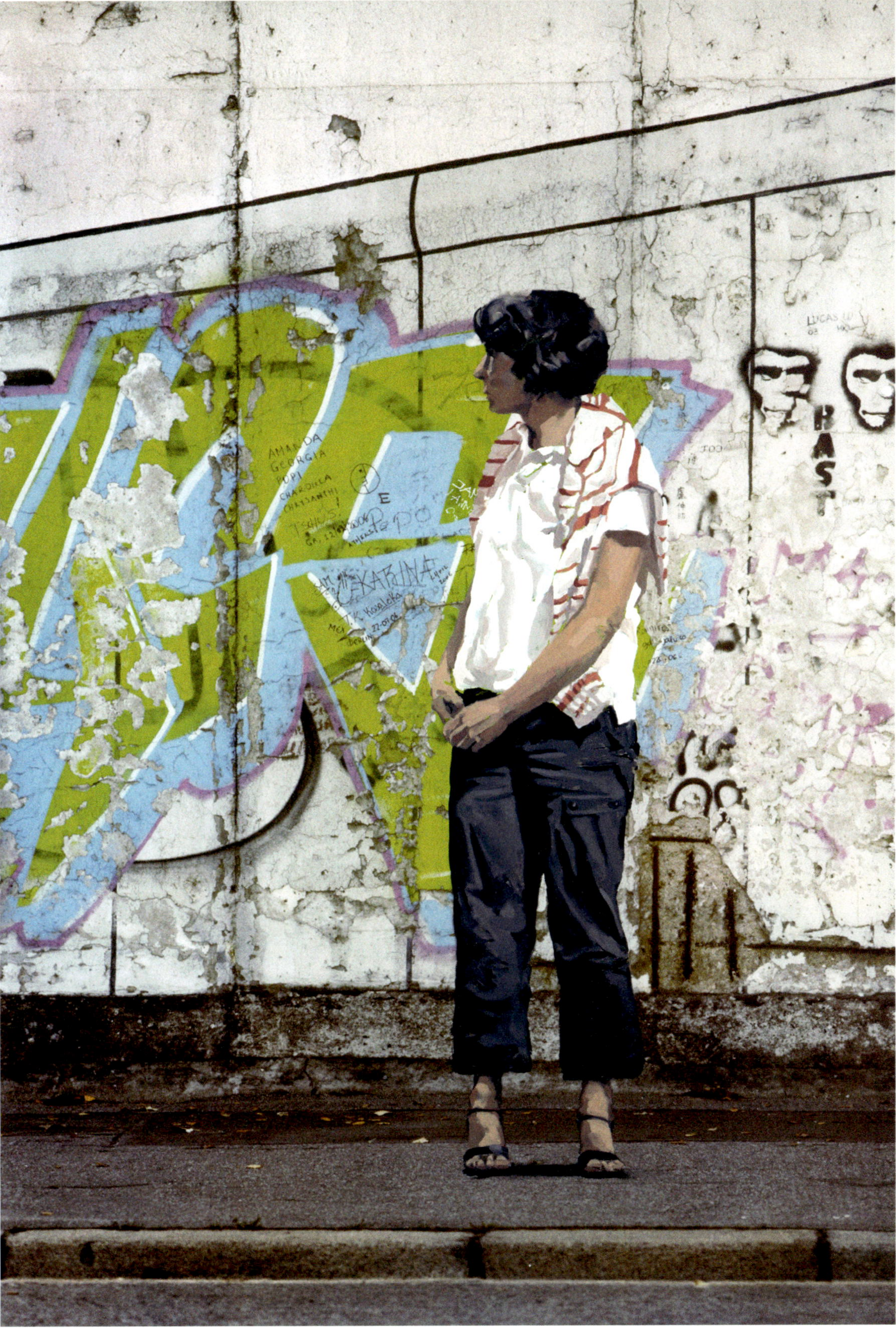

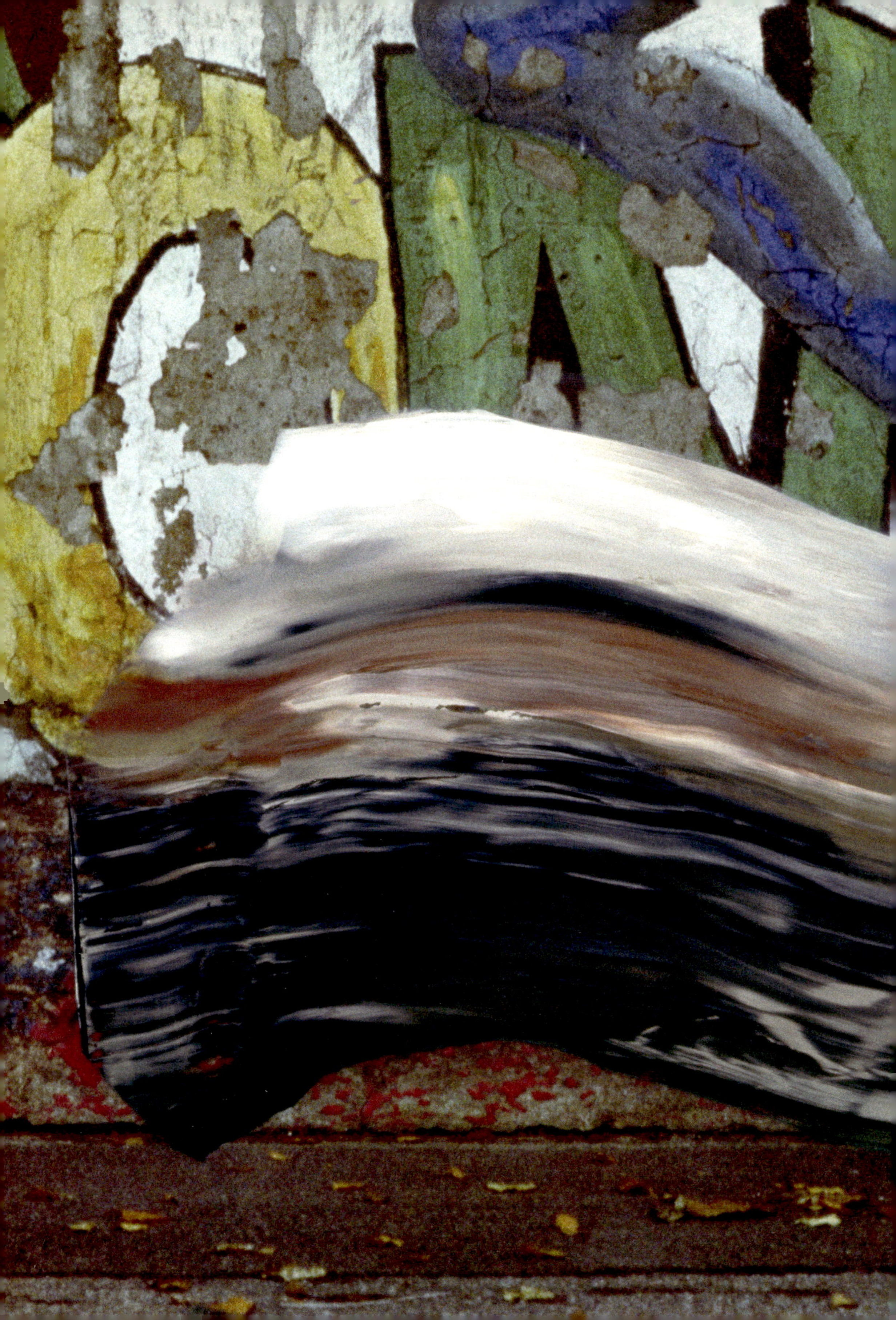

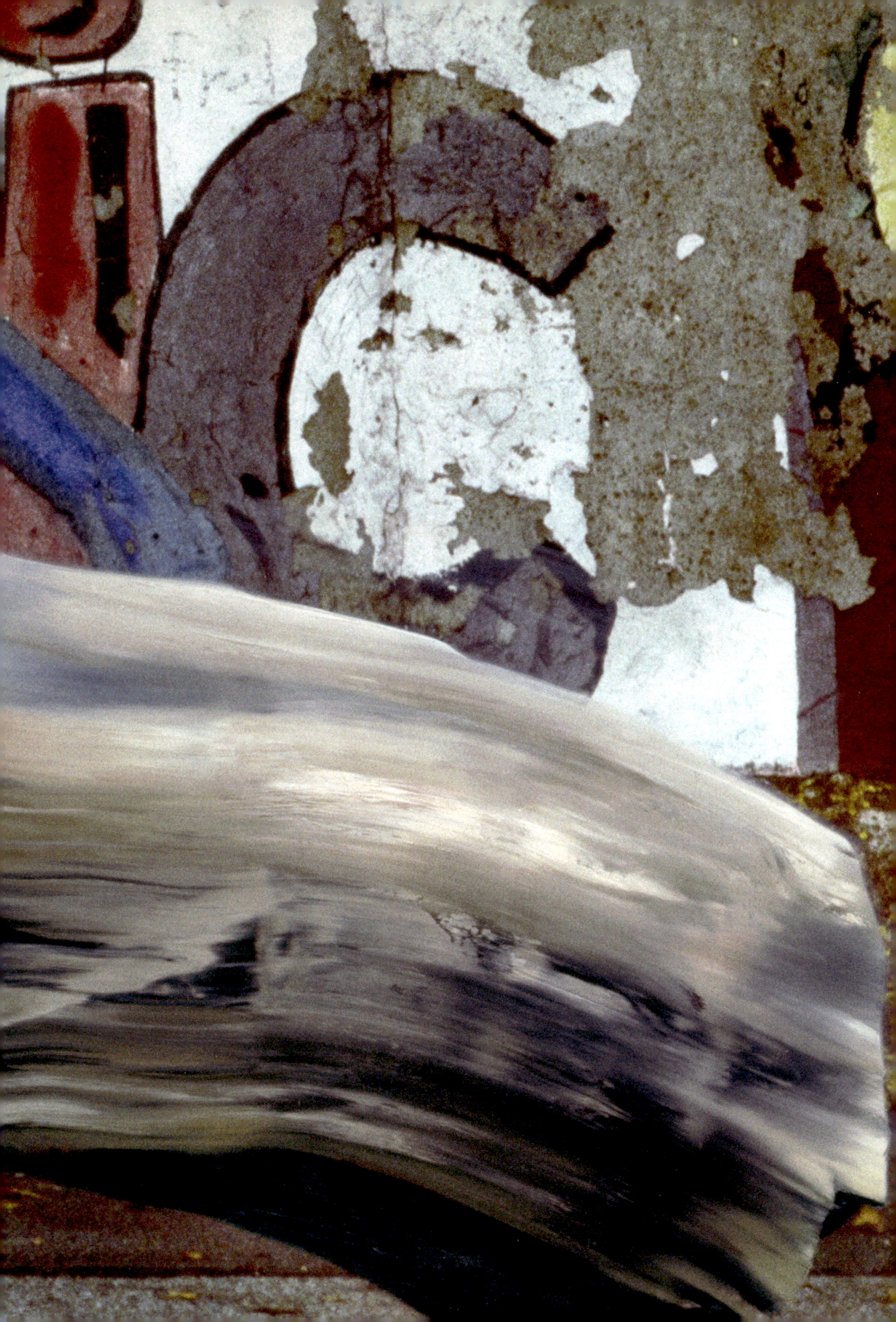

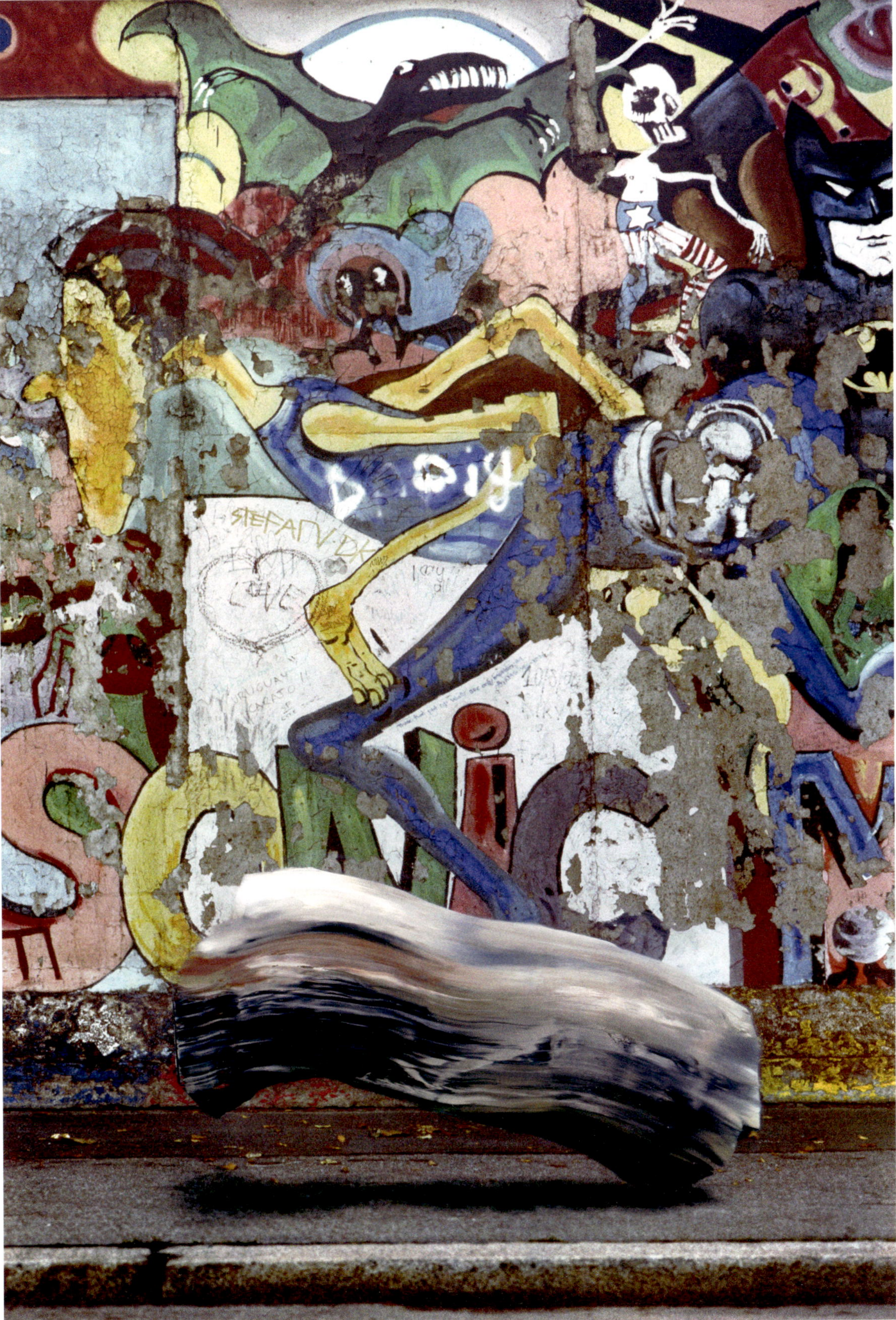

STEFAN DR
LOVE
URUGUAY
SCANIC

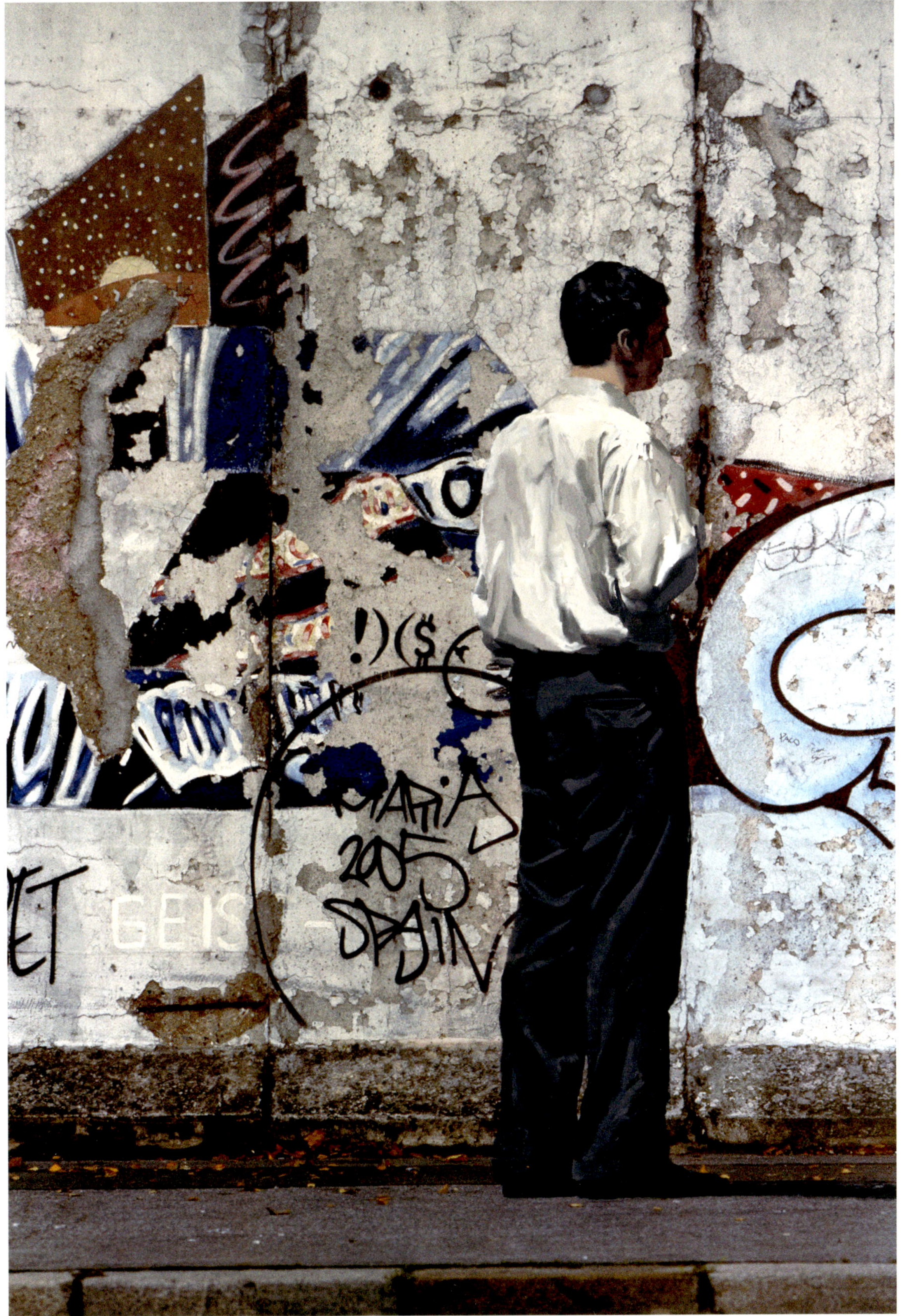

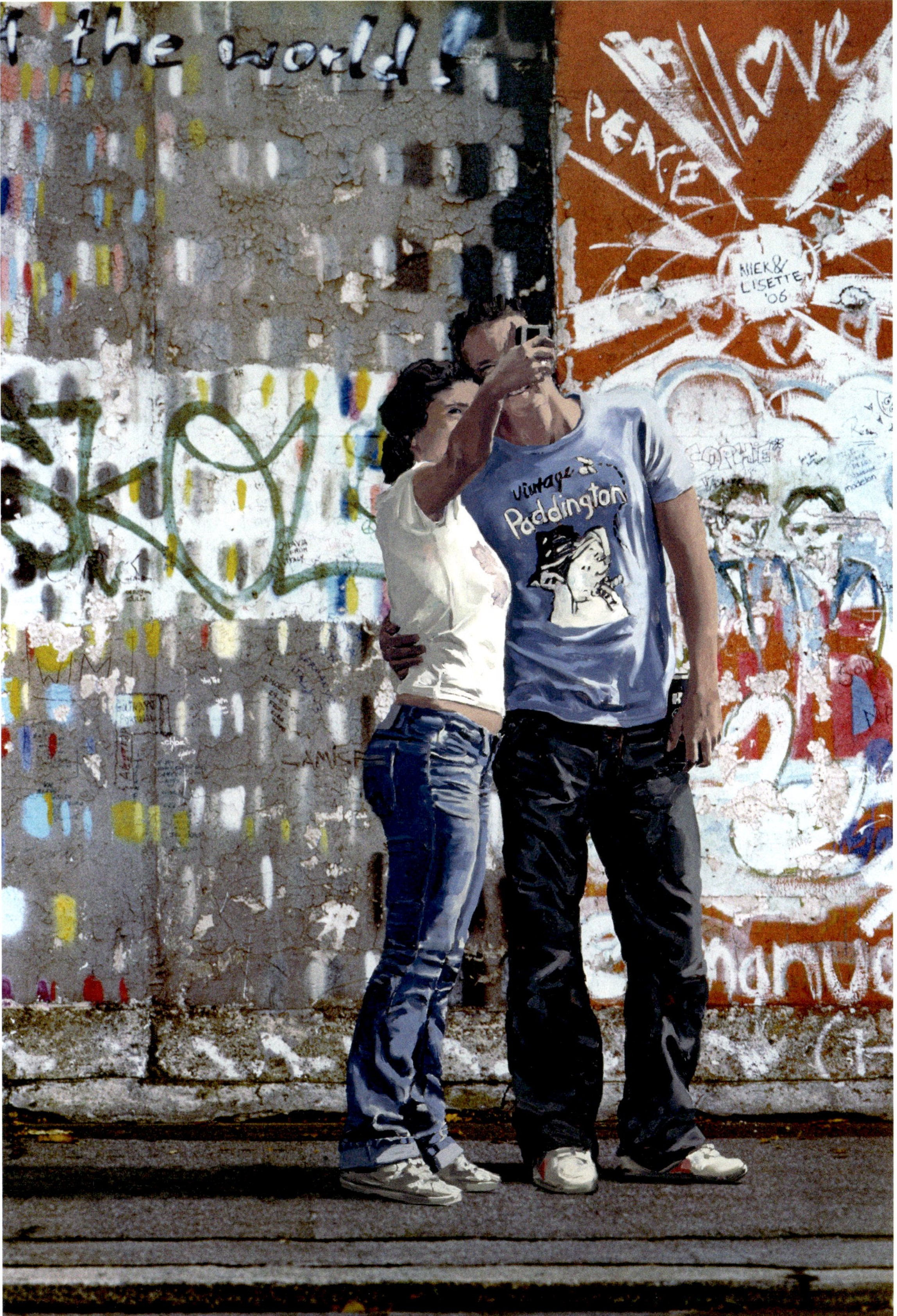
f the world!
PEACE LOVE
NIEK &
LISETTE
'06
Vintage
Paddington

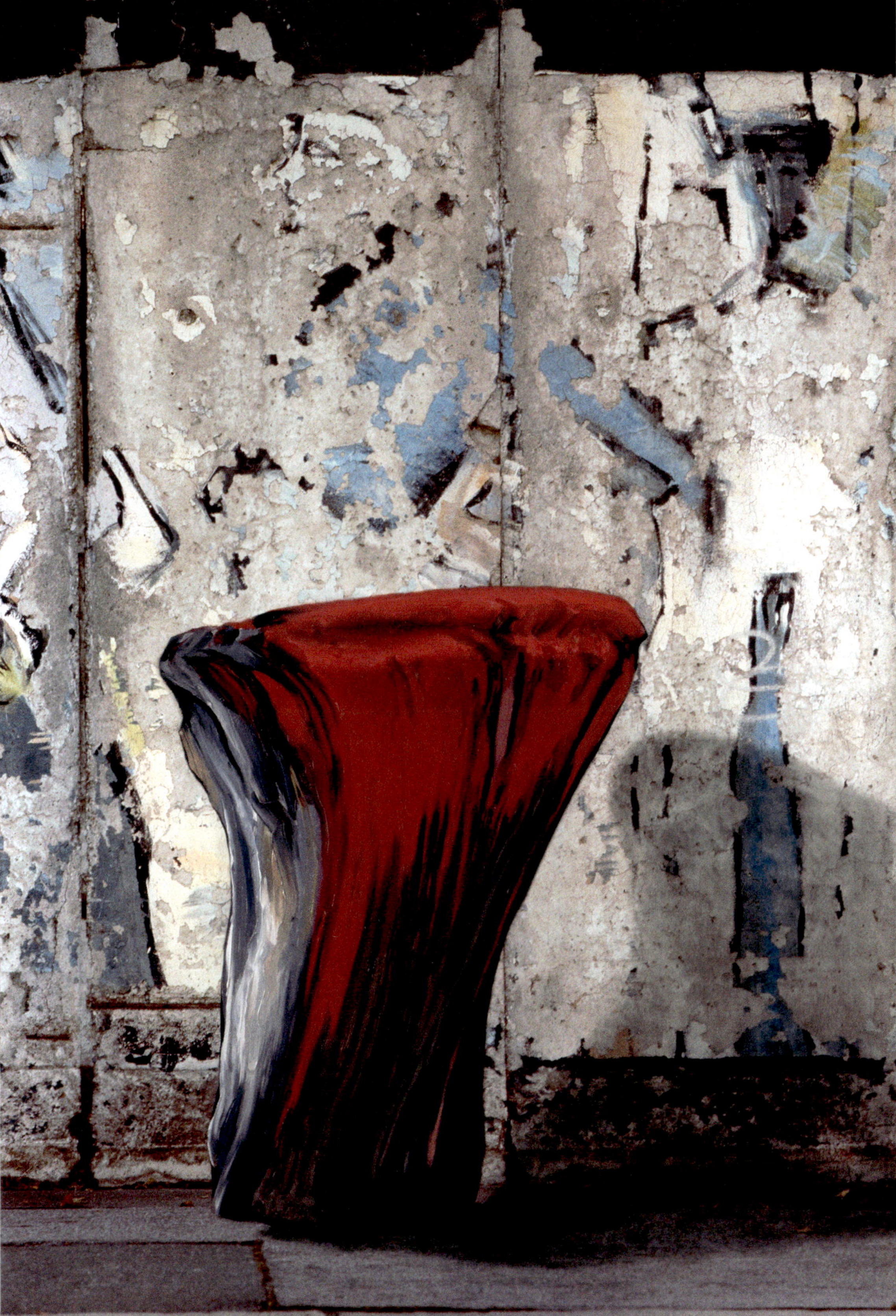

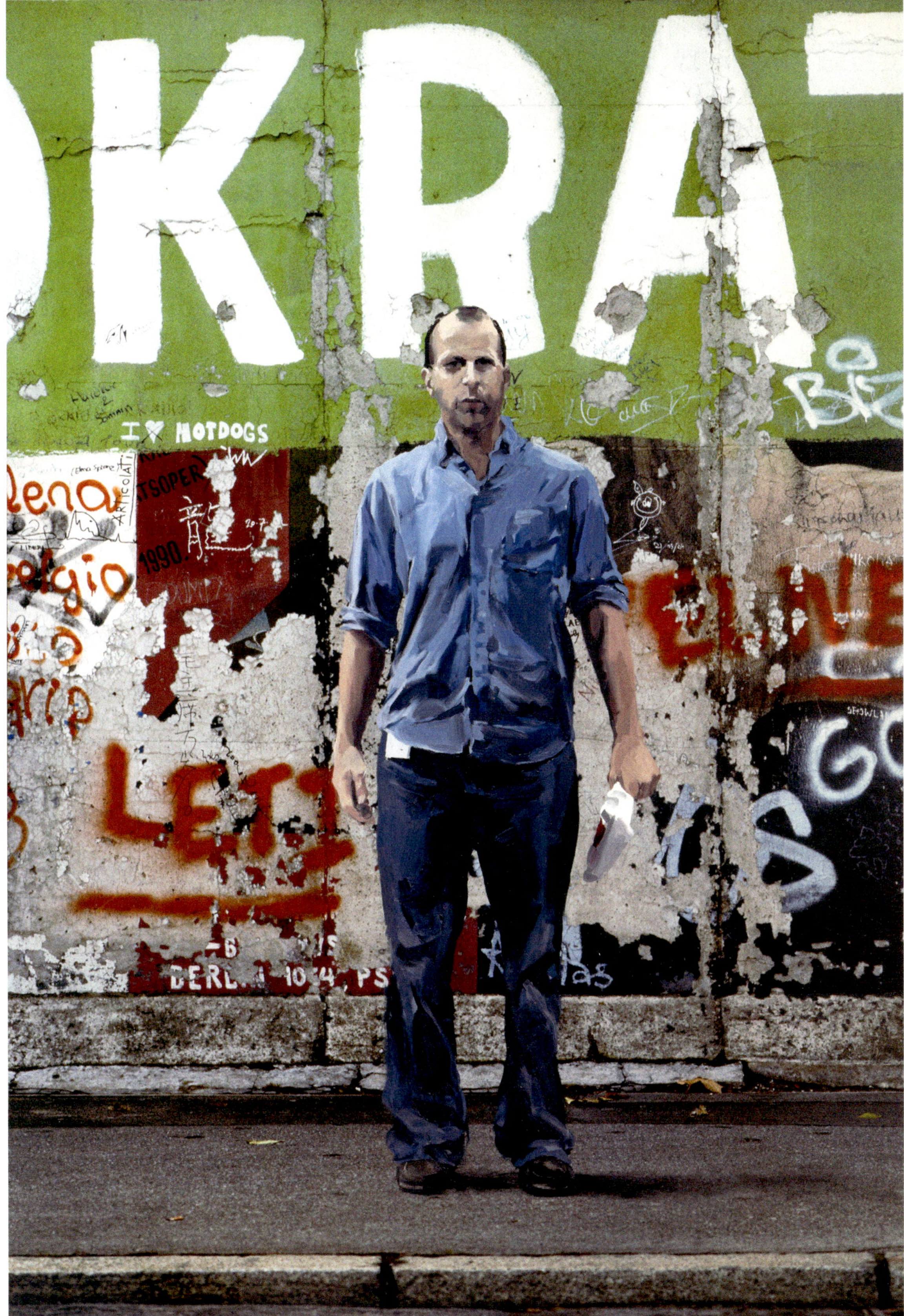

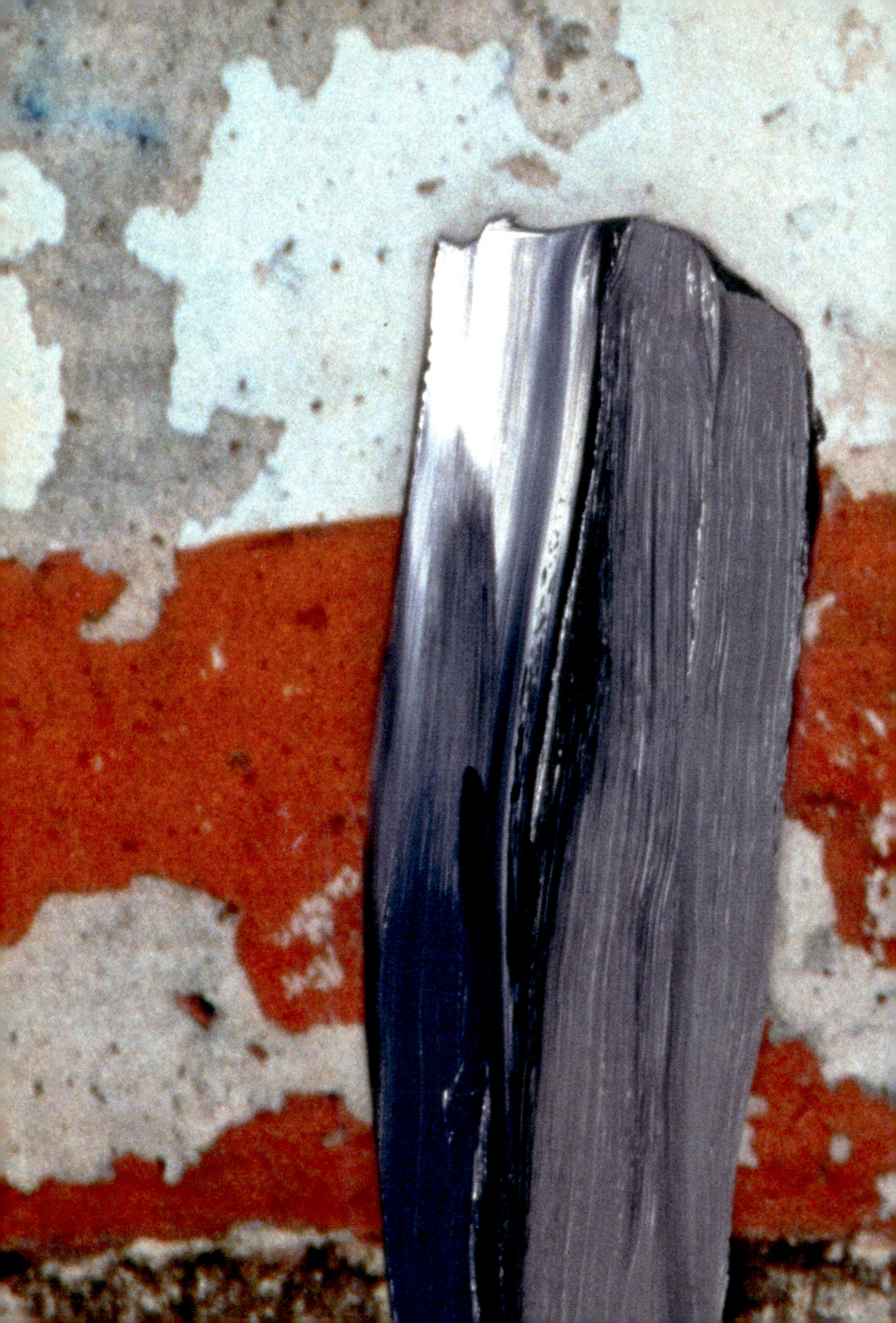

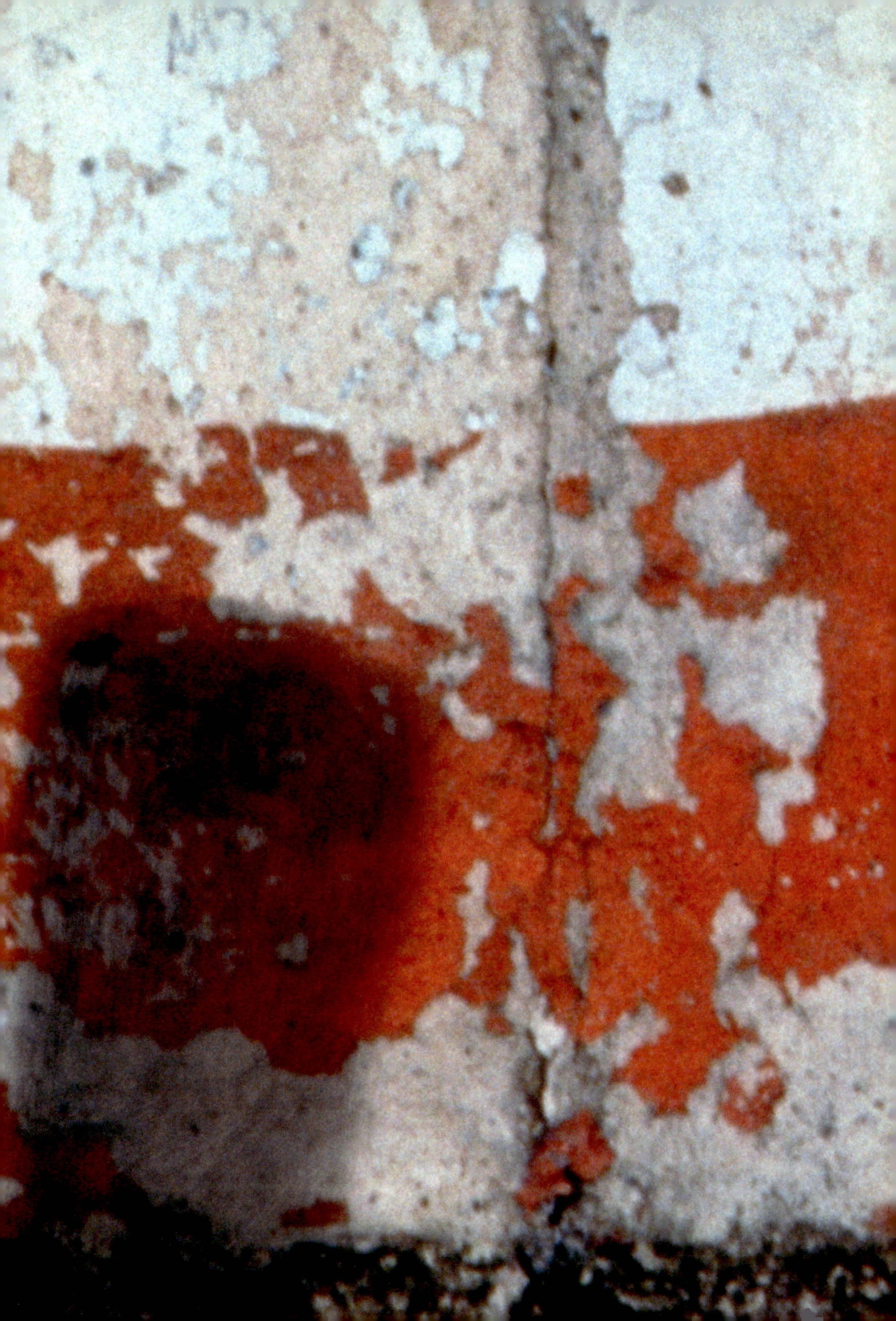

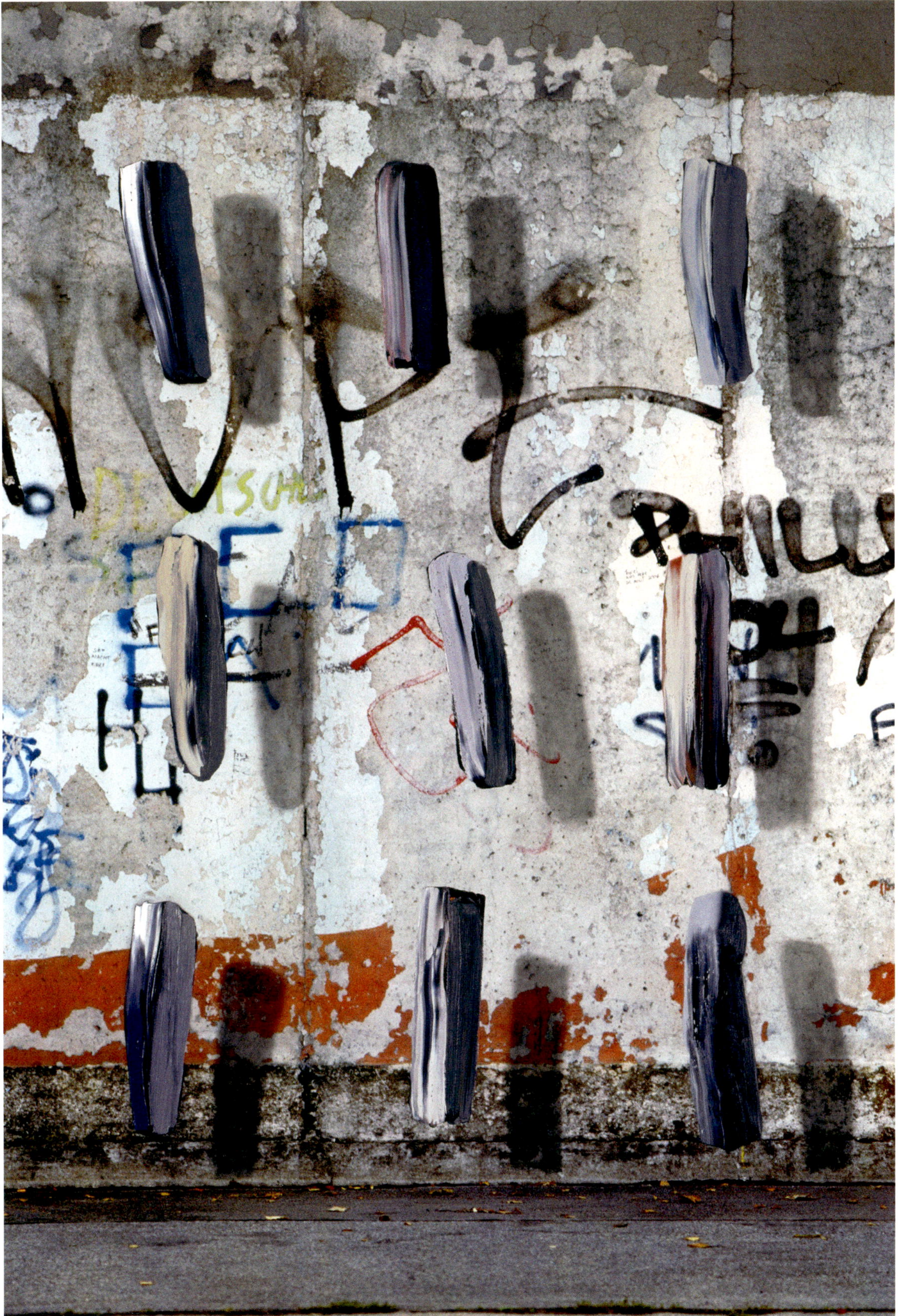

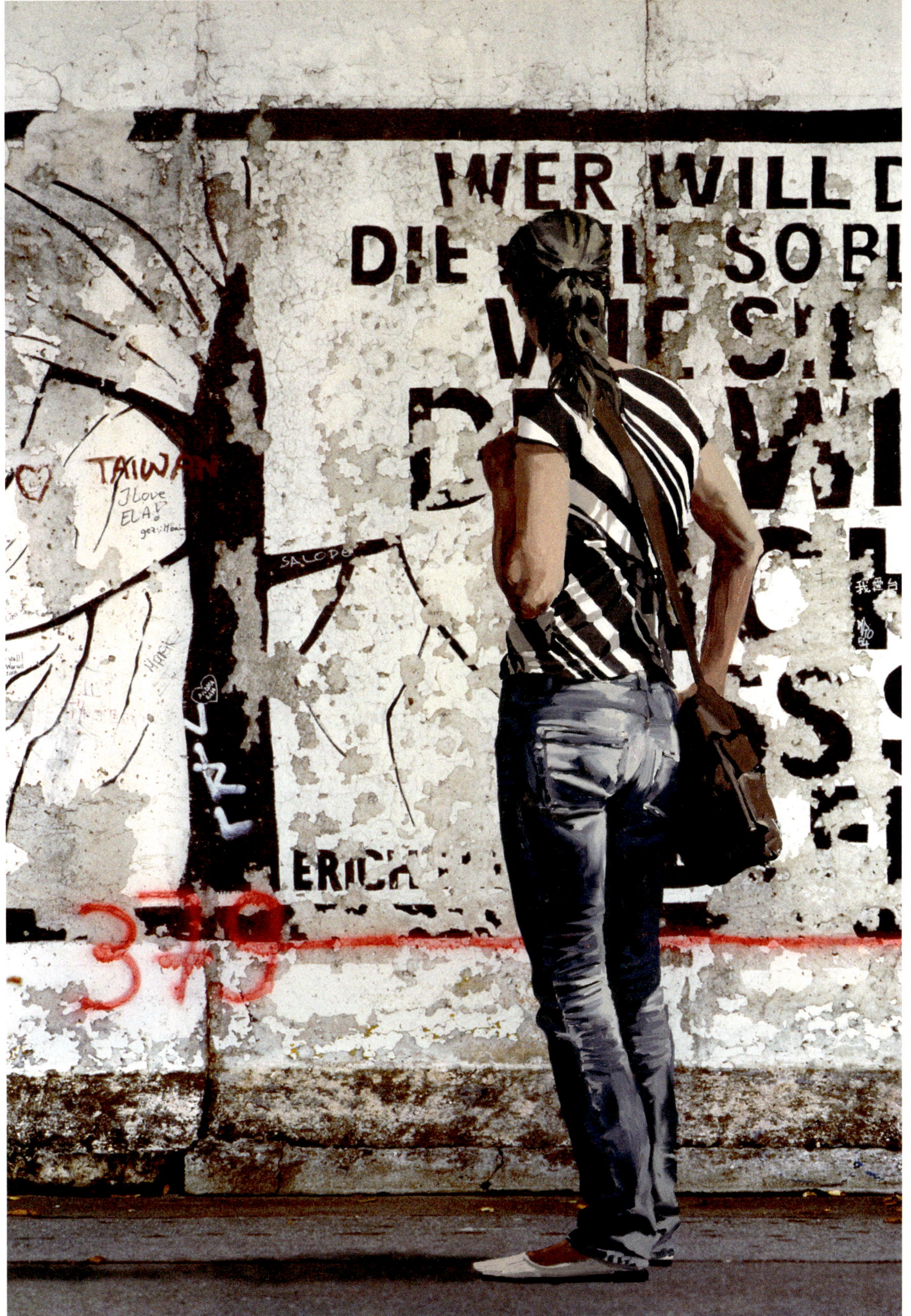

WER WILL D
DIE ILL SOB
WIE S
WI
TAIWAN
I Love
ELA
ERICH
370

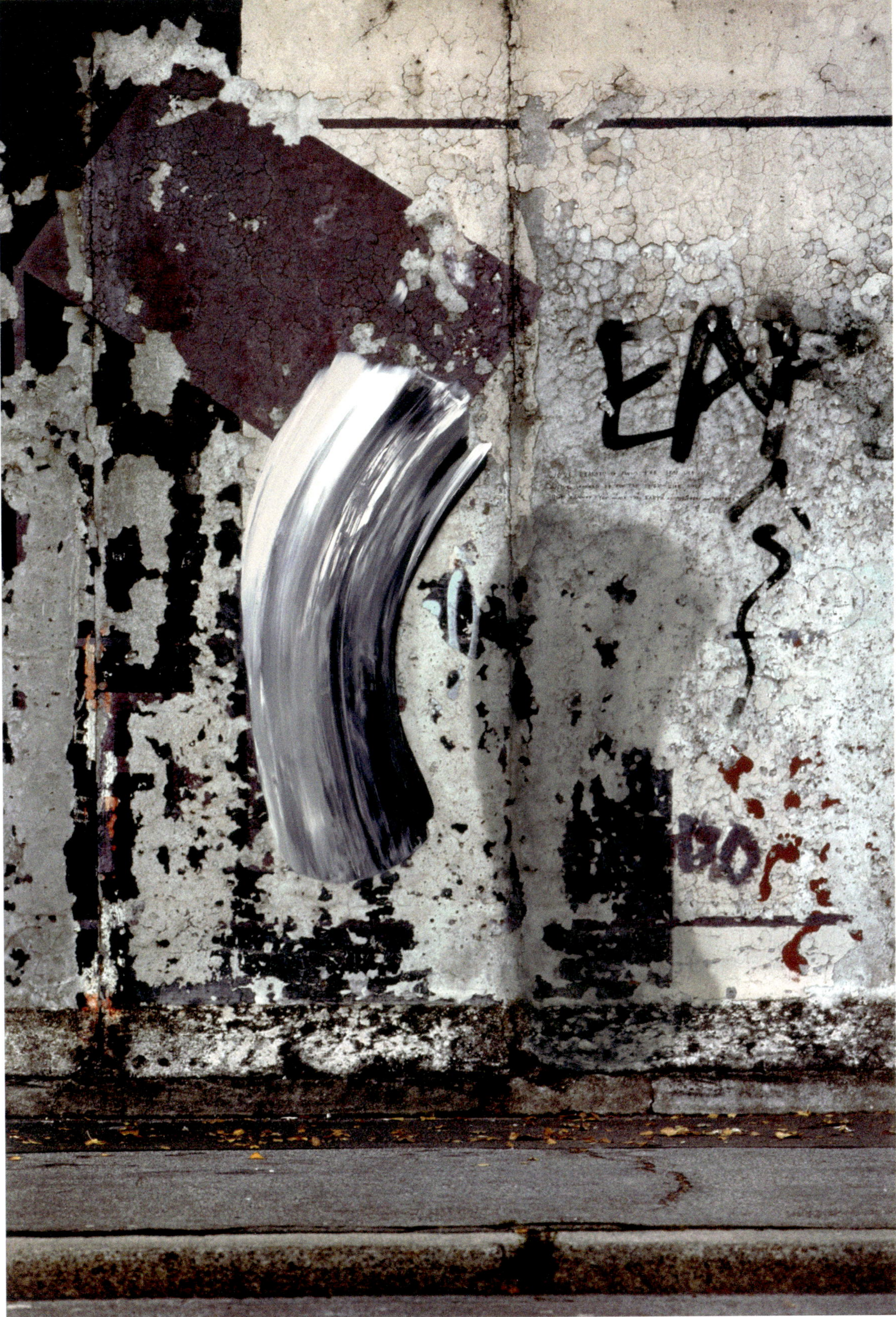
EAT

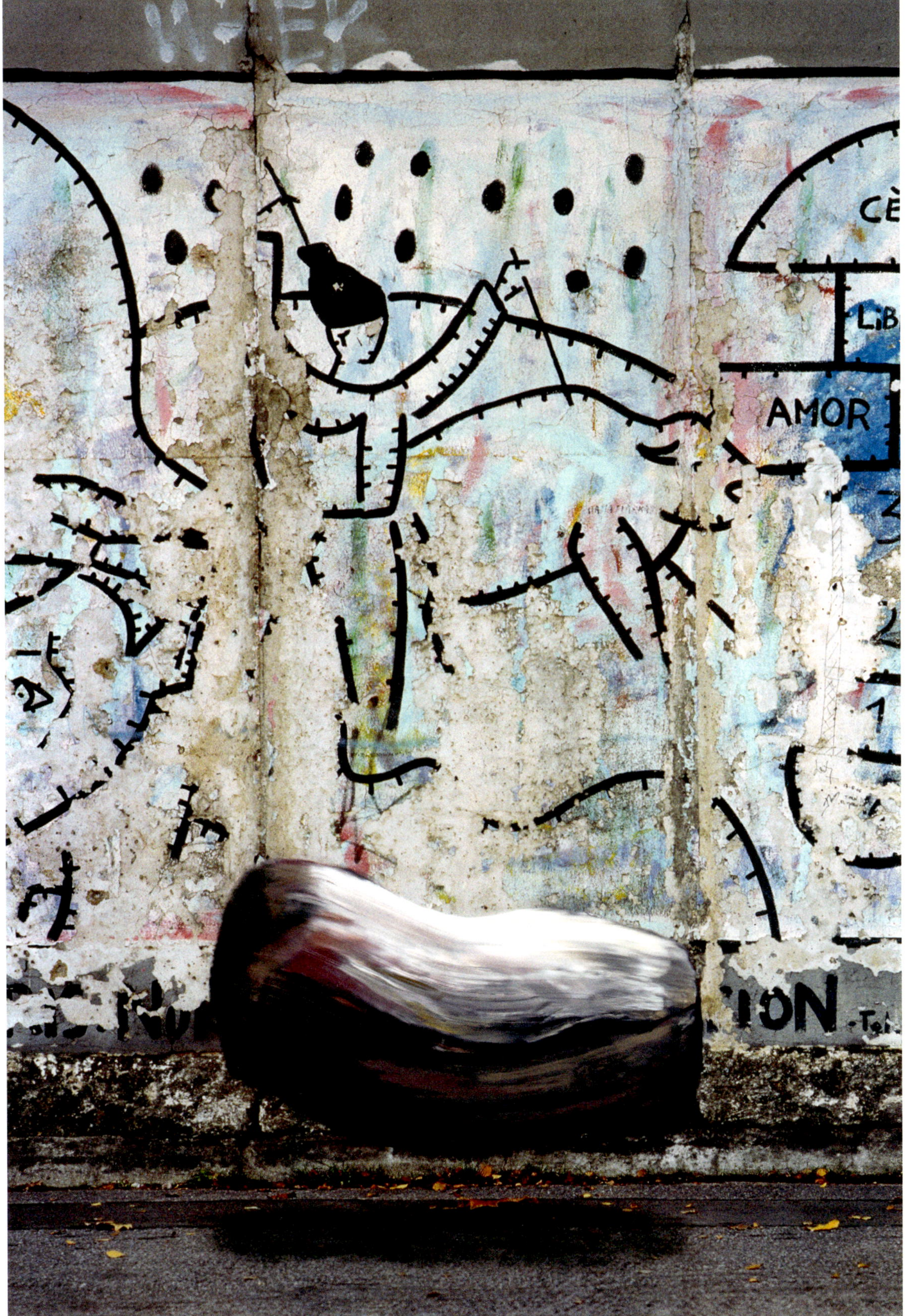
CÈ
LIB
AMOR
ION .Tel

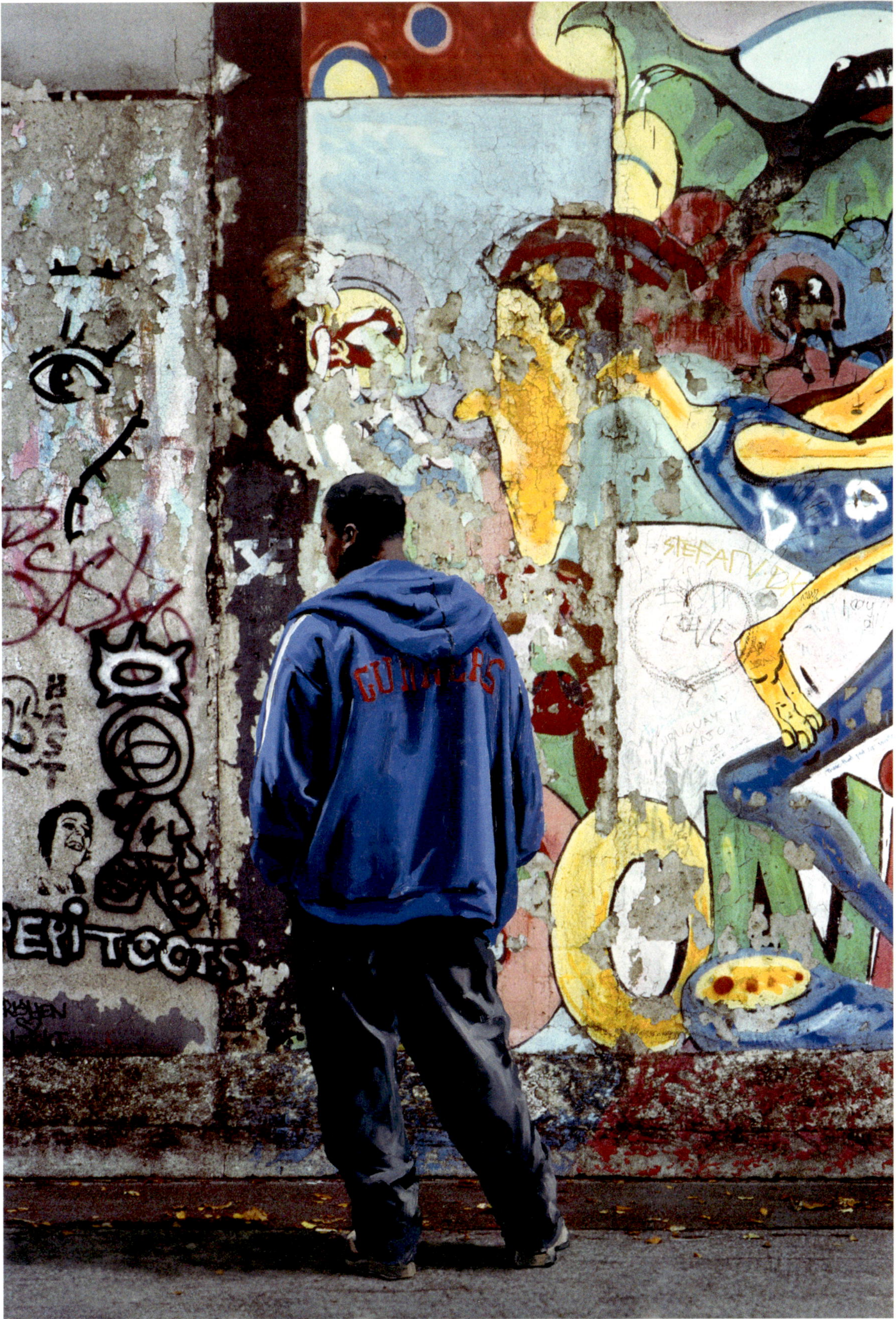

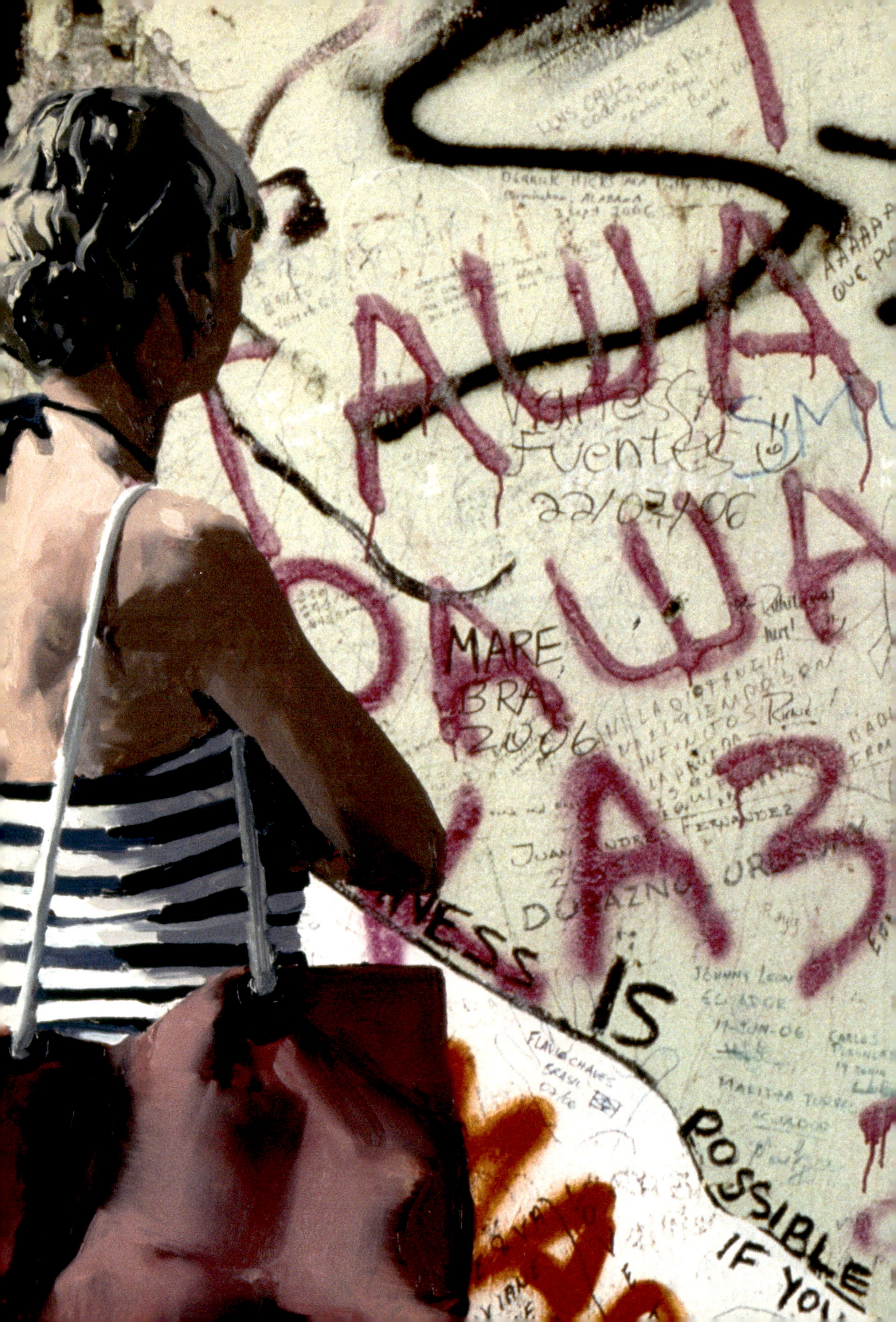
AWA
Vanessa
Fuentes
22/07/06
MARE
BRA
2006
NESS IS
POSSIBLE
IF YOU

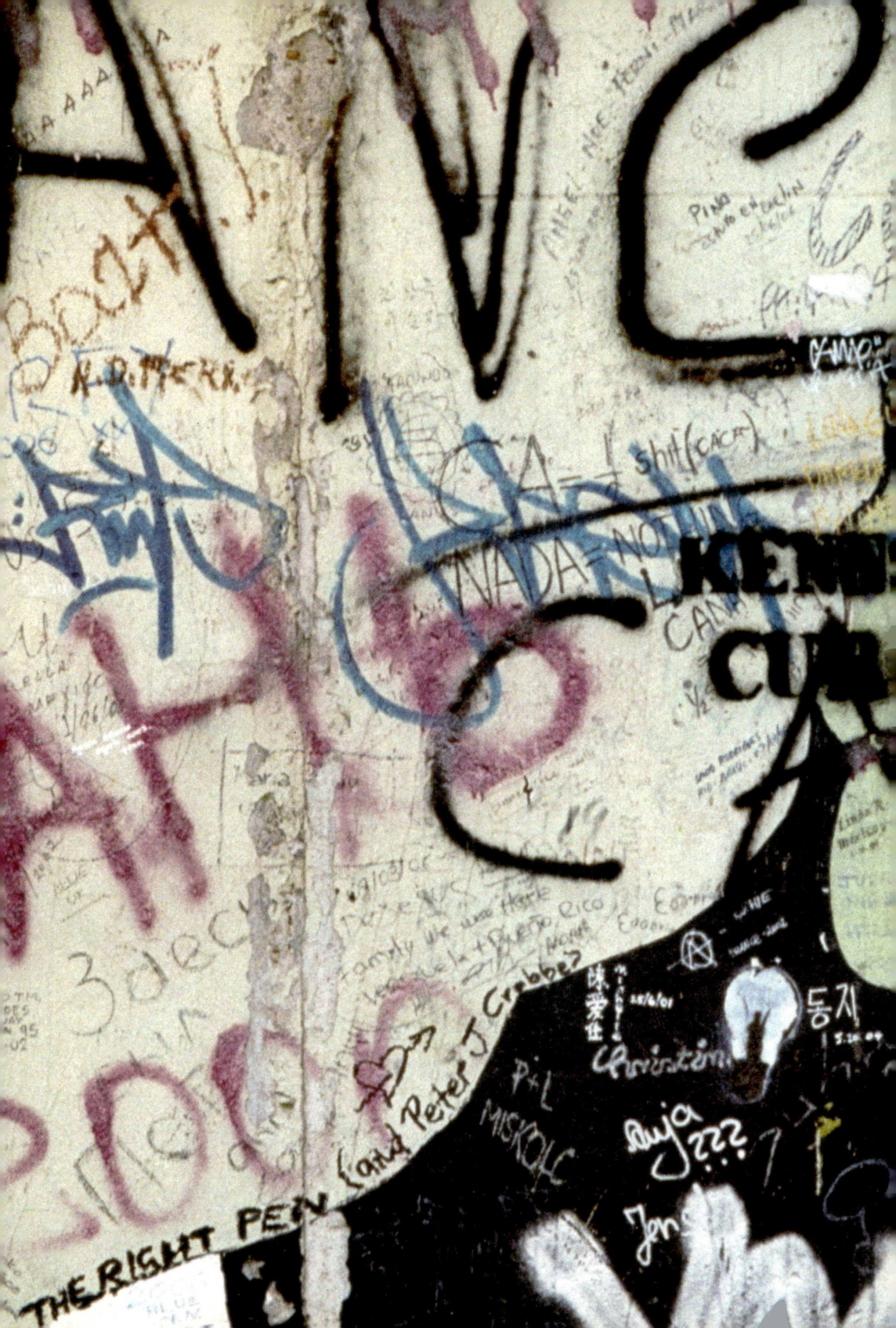

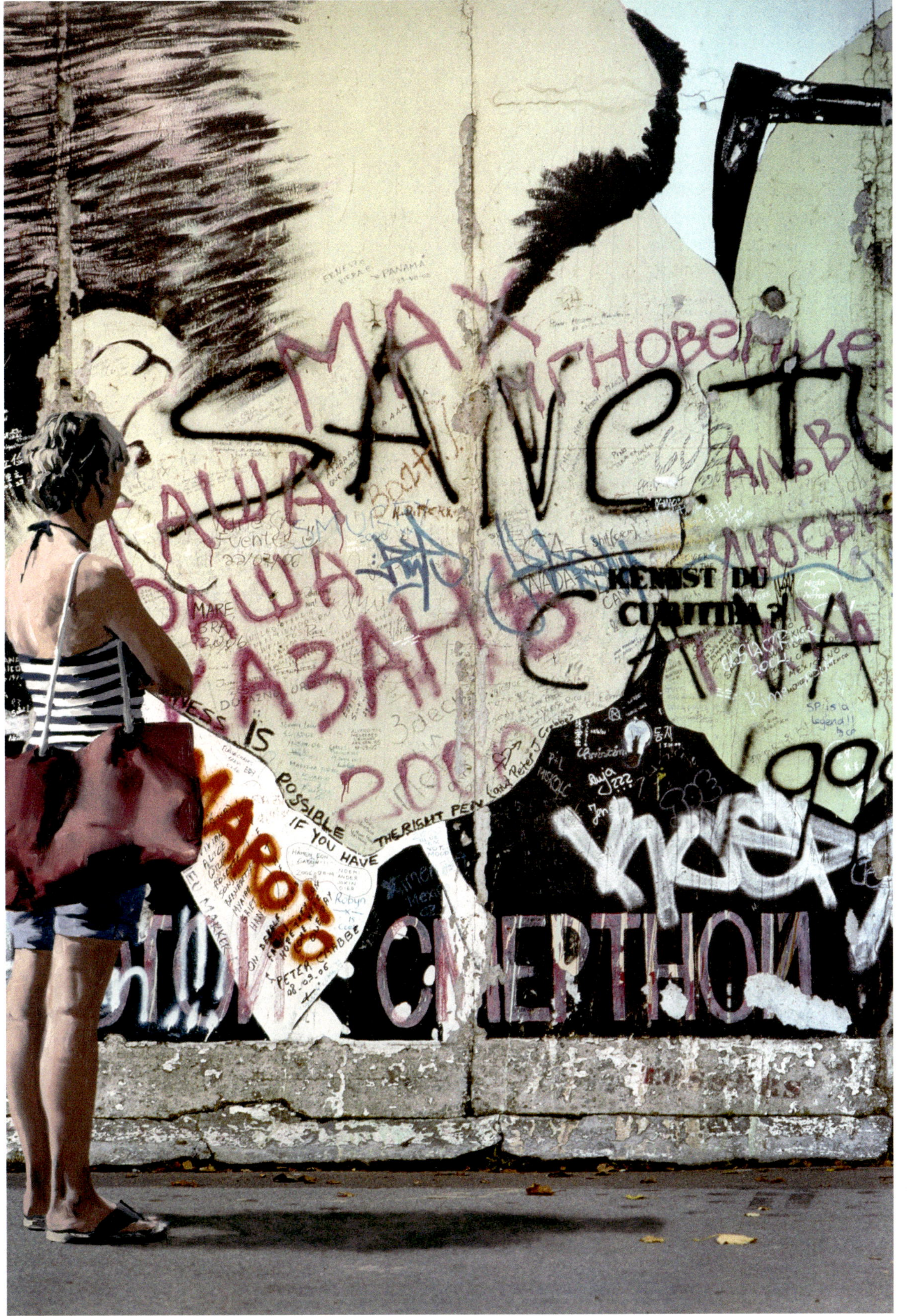

MAX
SAVE
KENST DU
CURITIBA?
MAROTO
THE RIGHT PEN
BUSINESS IS
POSSIBLE
IF YOU HAVE
CMEPTHOIO

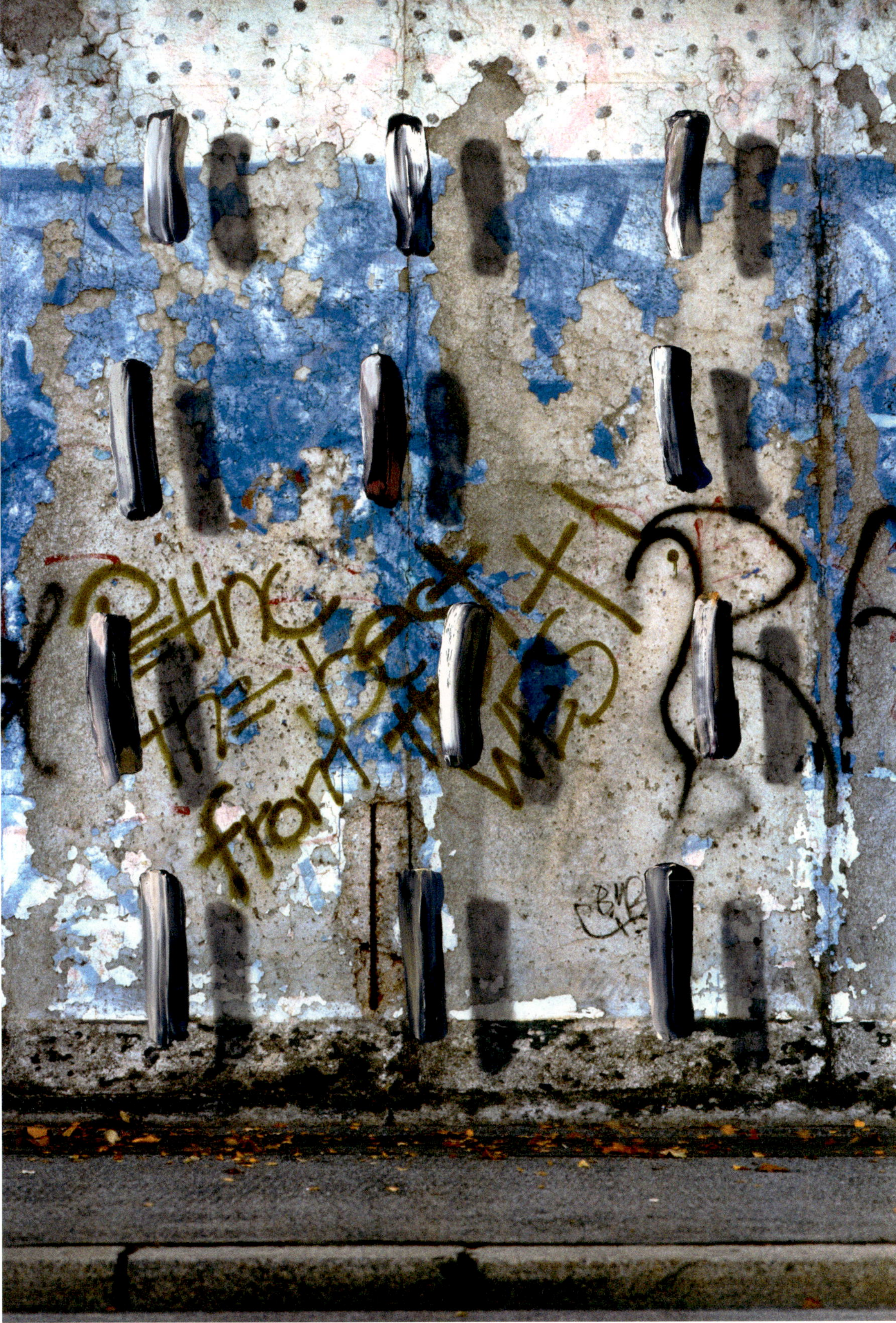
frei
West

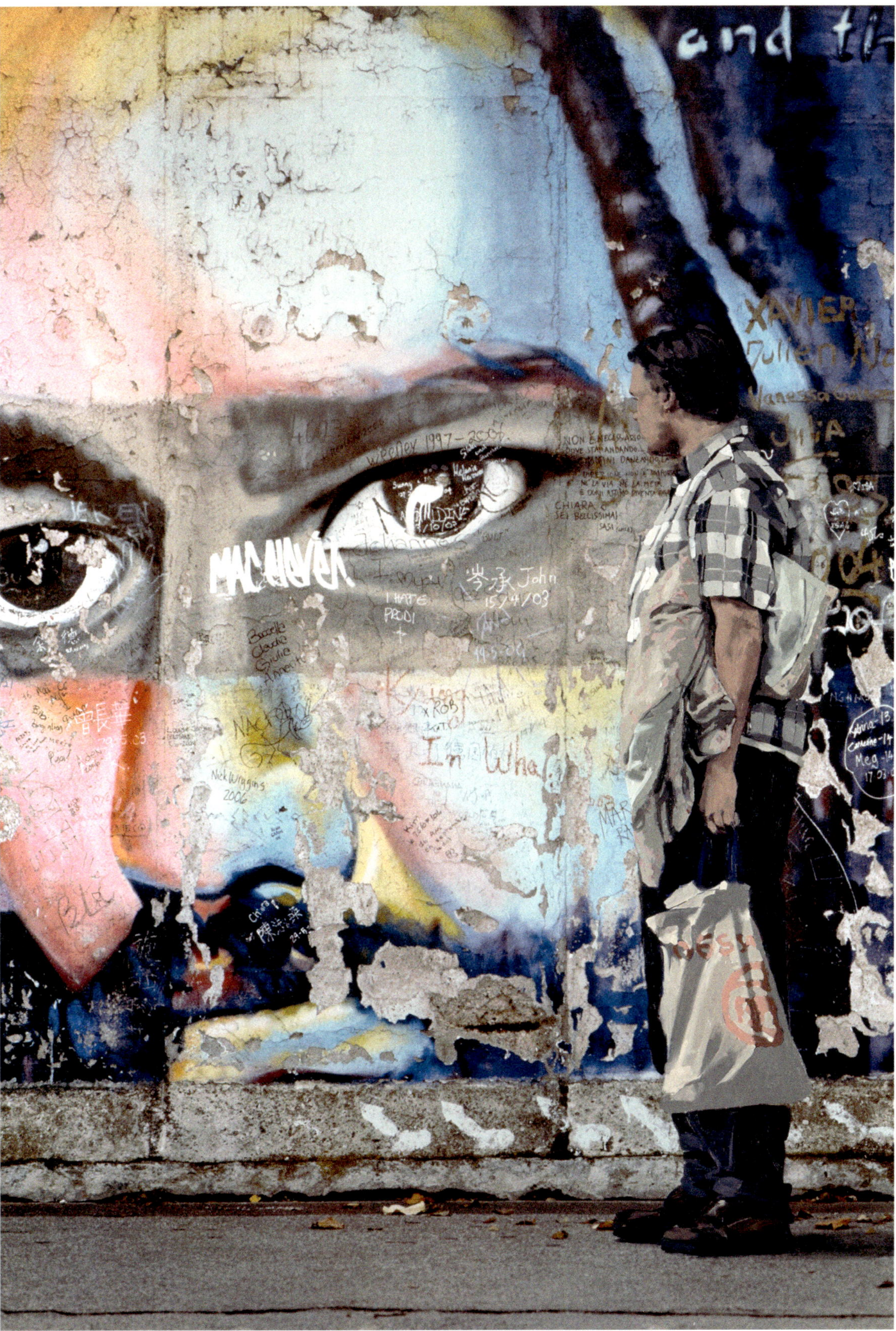

and th
MAC UAVER
weeney 1997-200
XAVIER
Julien
Vanessa
JULIA
NON E NECESSARIO
DOVE STAI ANDANDO
CHIARA
SEI BELLISSIMA!
SASA
李承 John
15/4/03
I HATE
PRODI
I n Wha.
Nick Wiggins
2006
MAR
RA
OESY

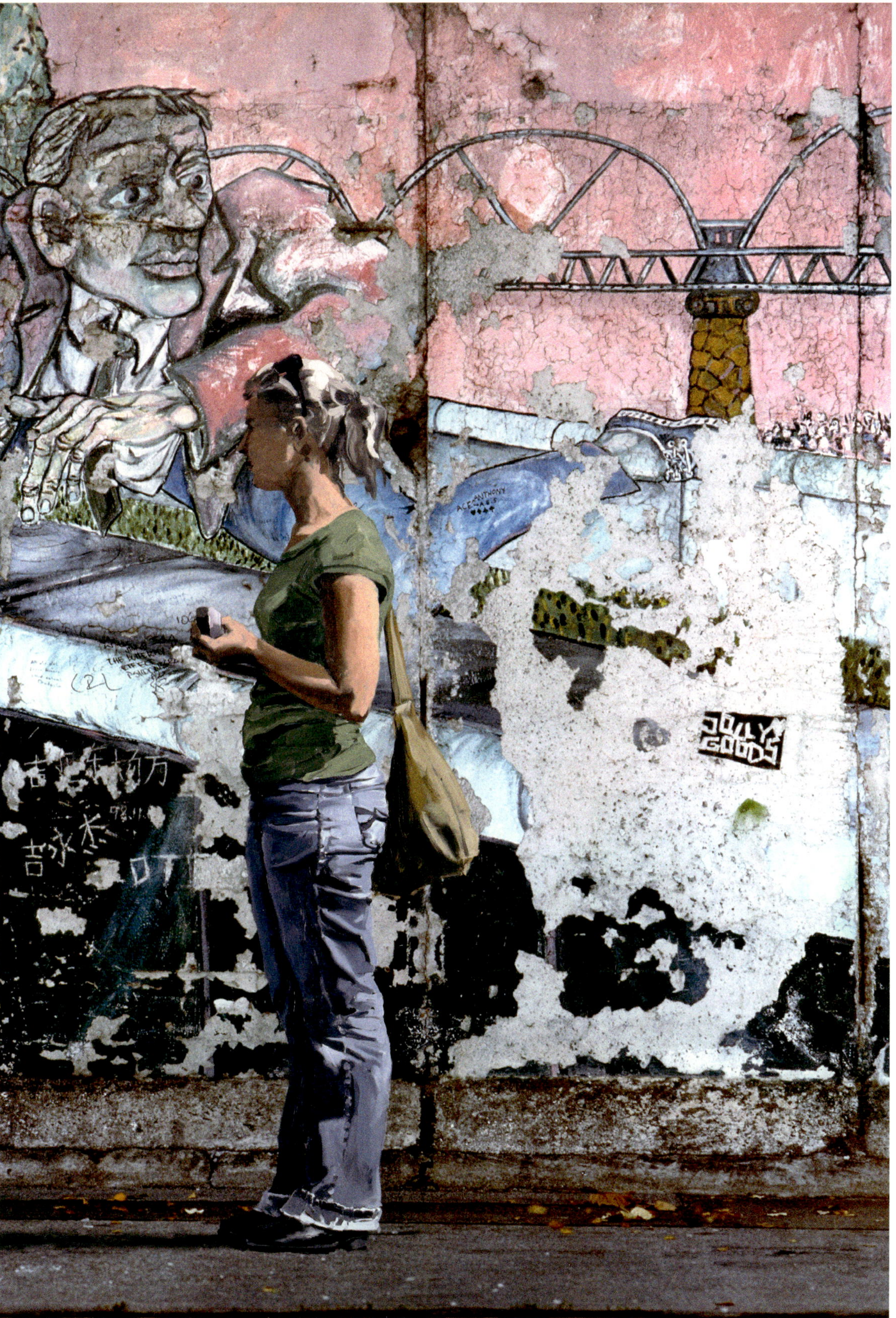

JOLLY
GOODS

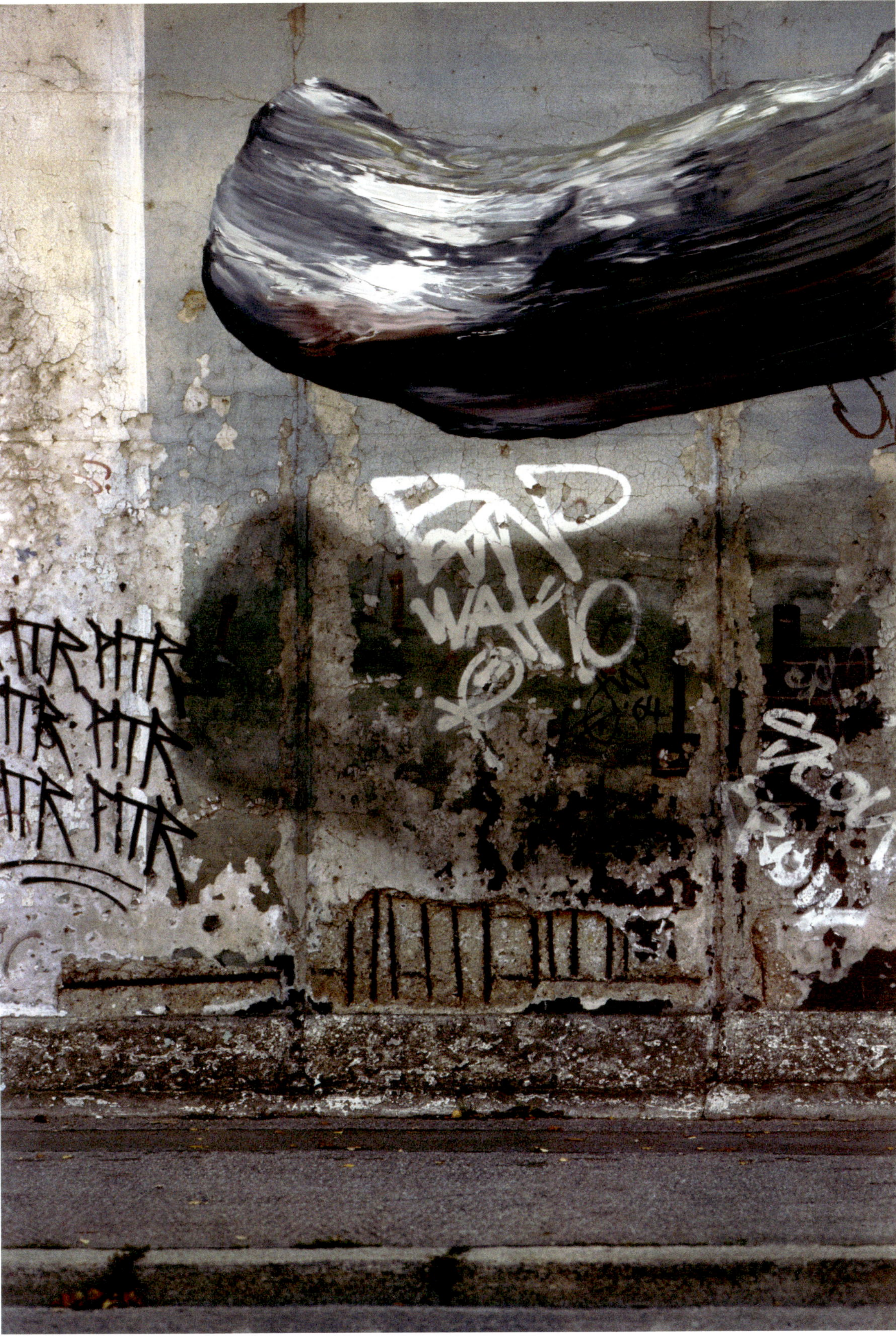

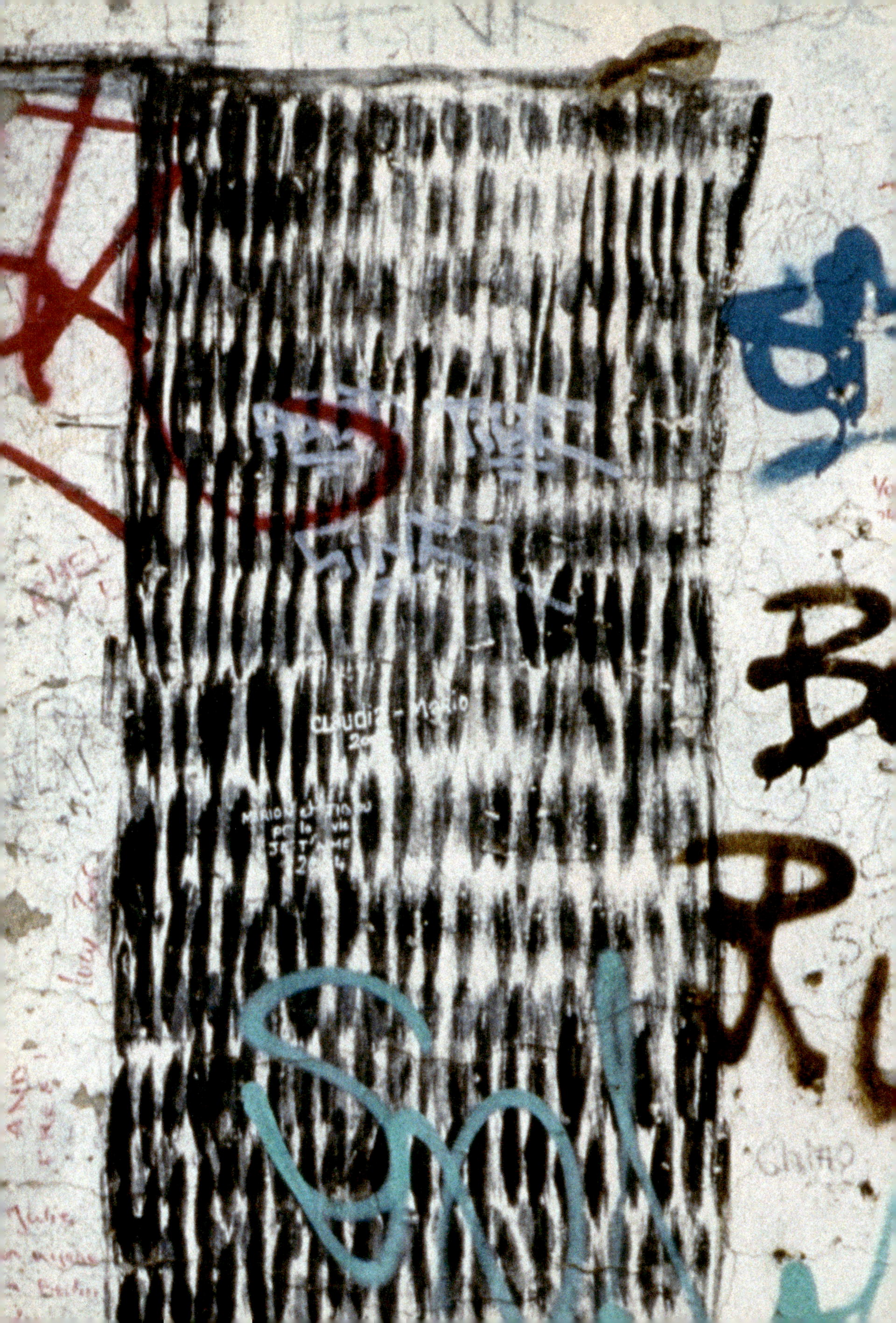

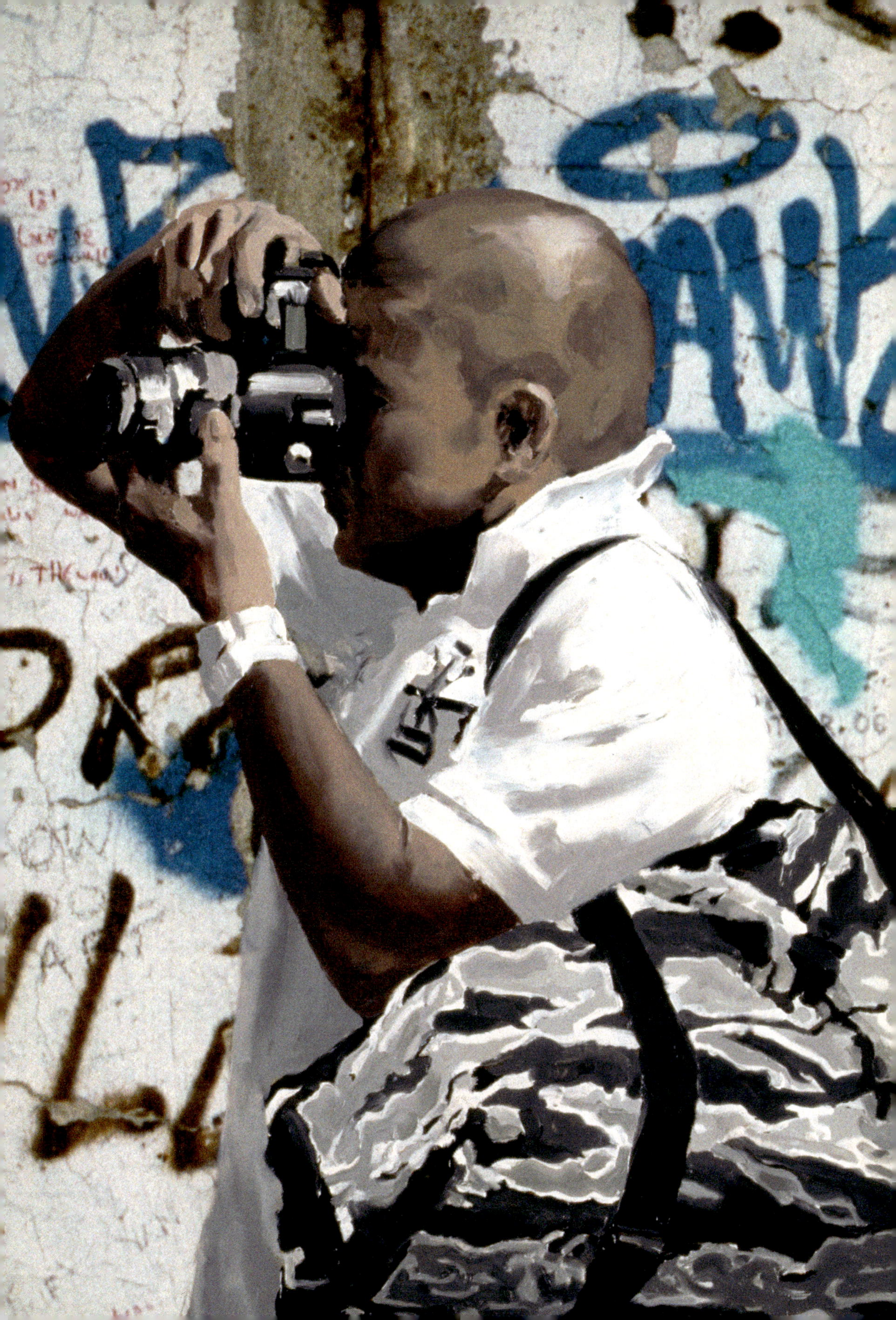

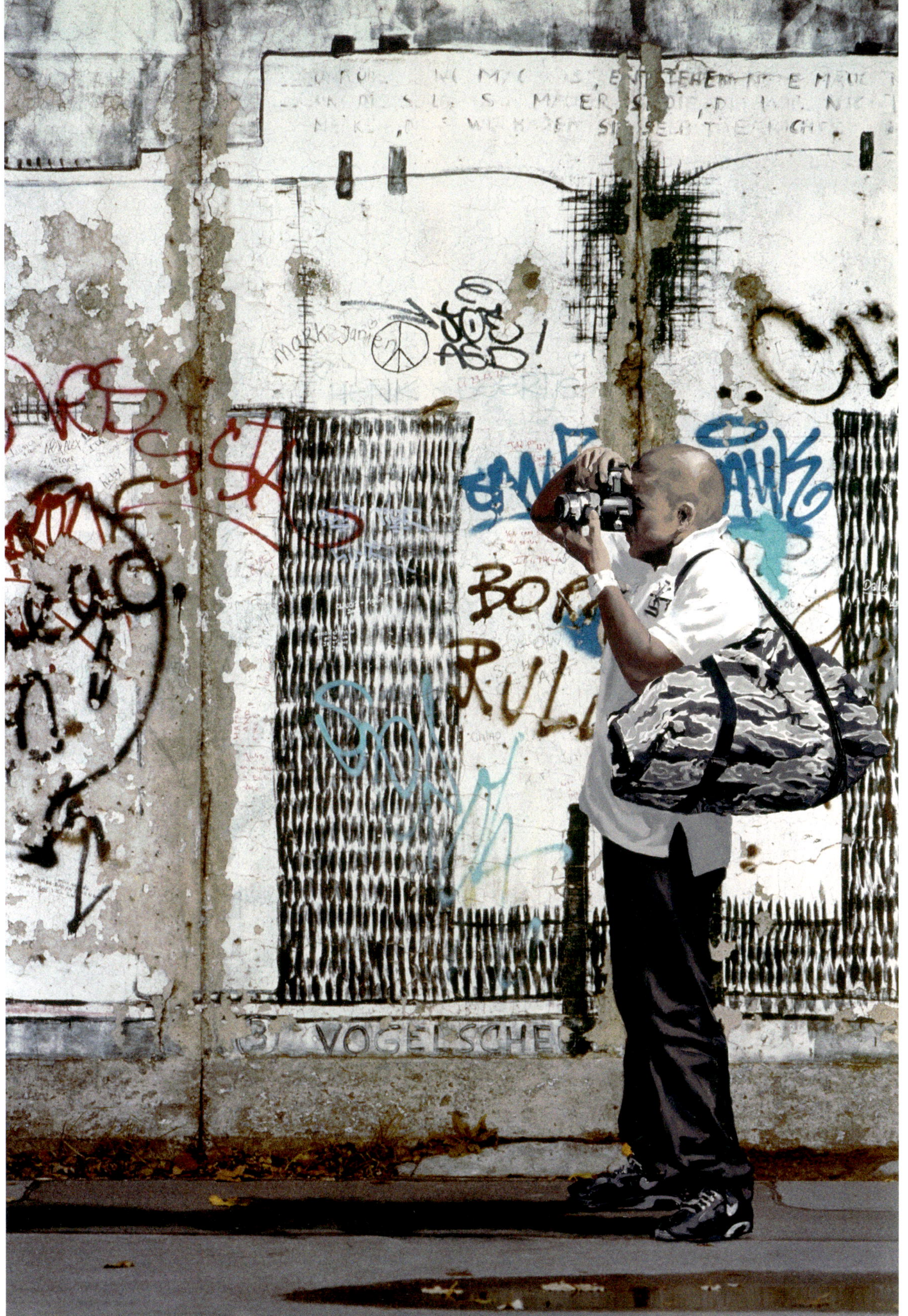

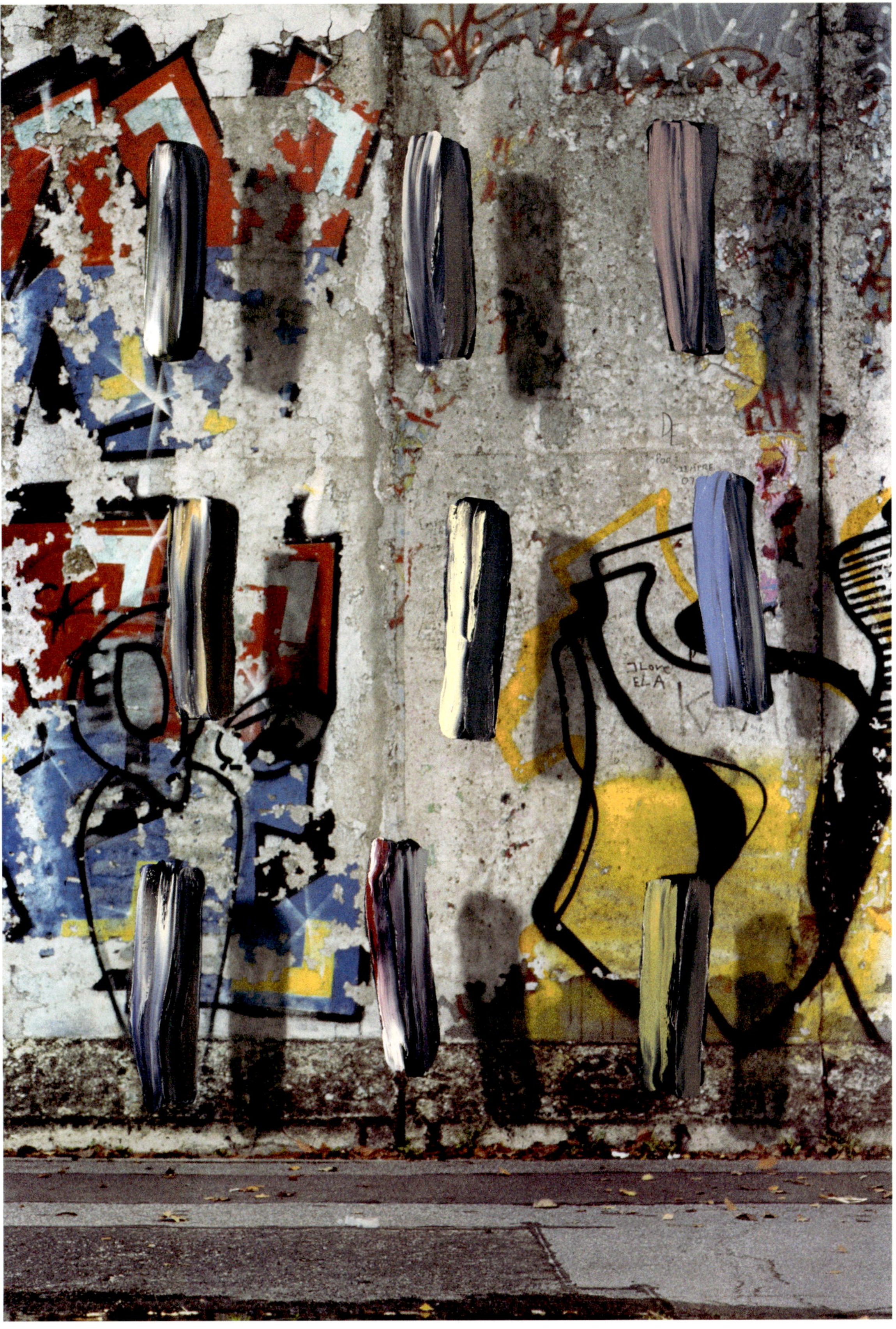

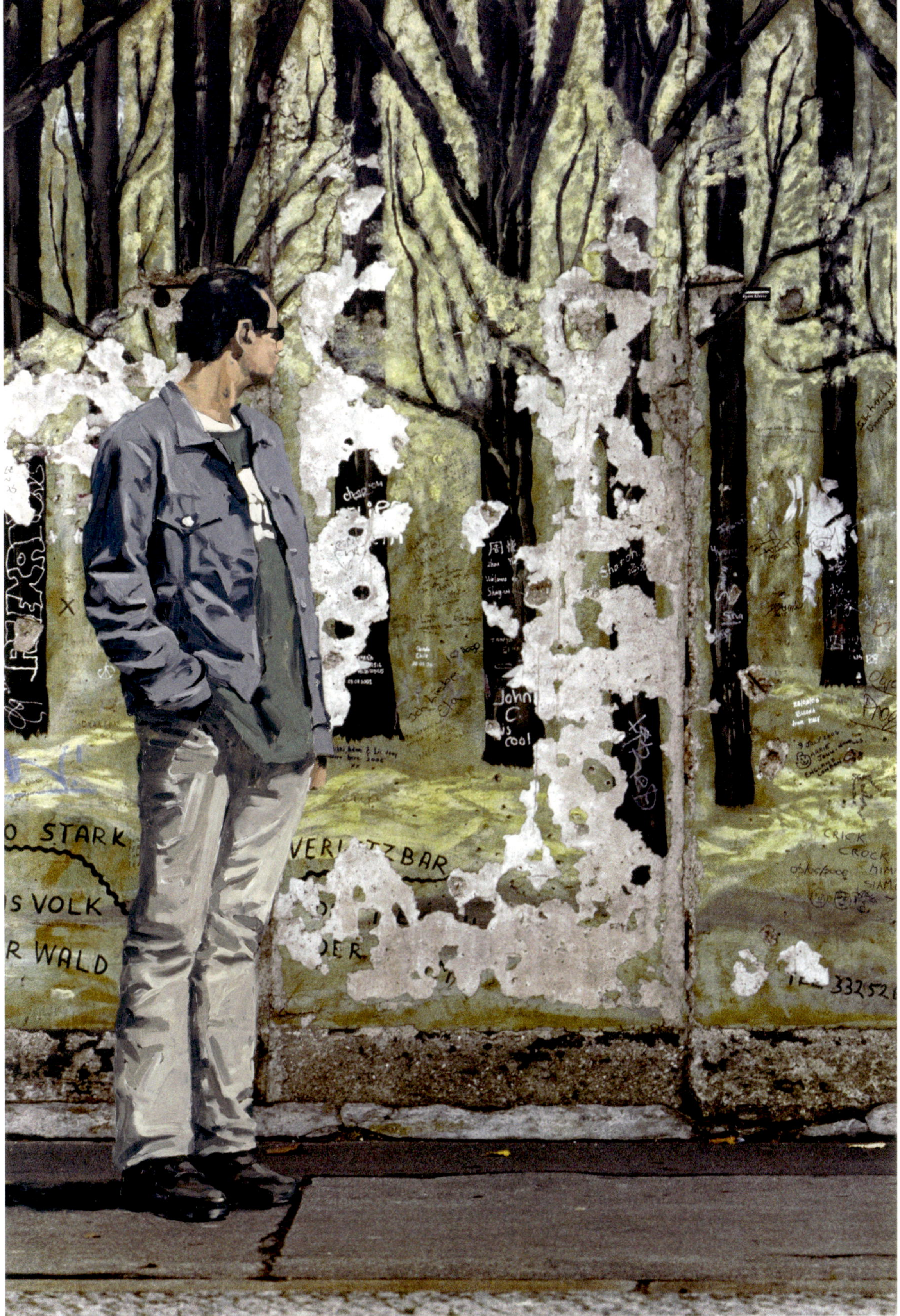
O STARK
VERLETZBAR
S VOLK
R WALD
1L-332.52

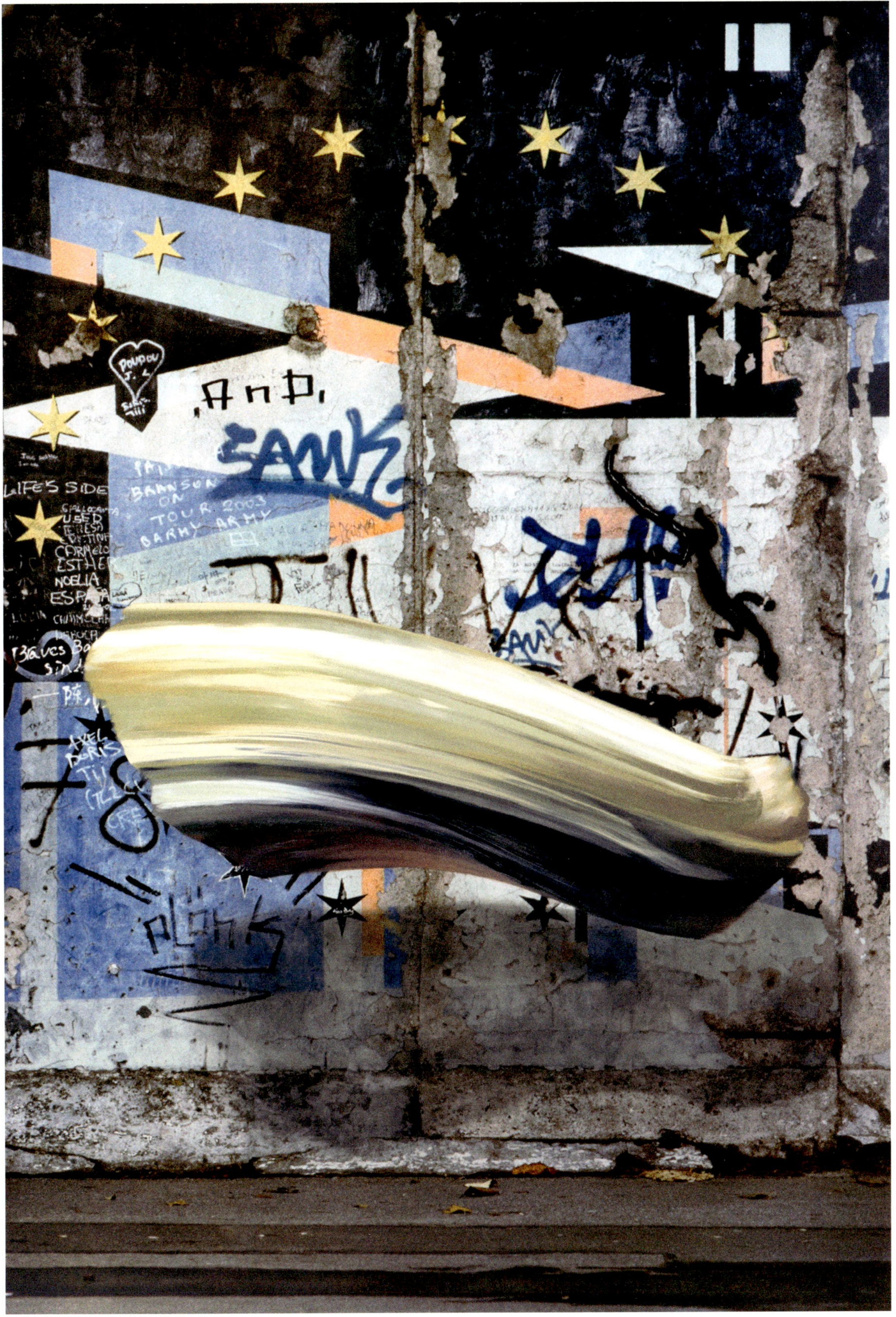

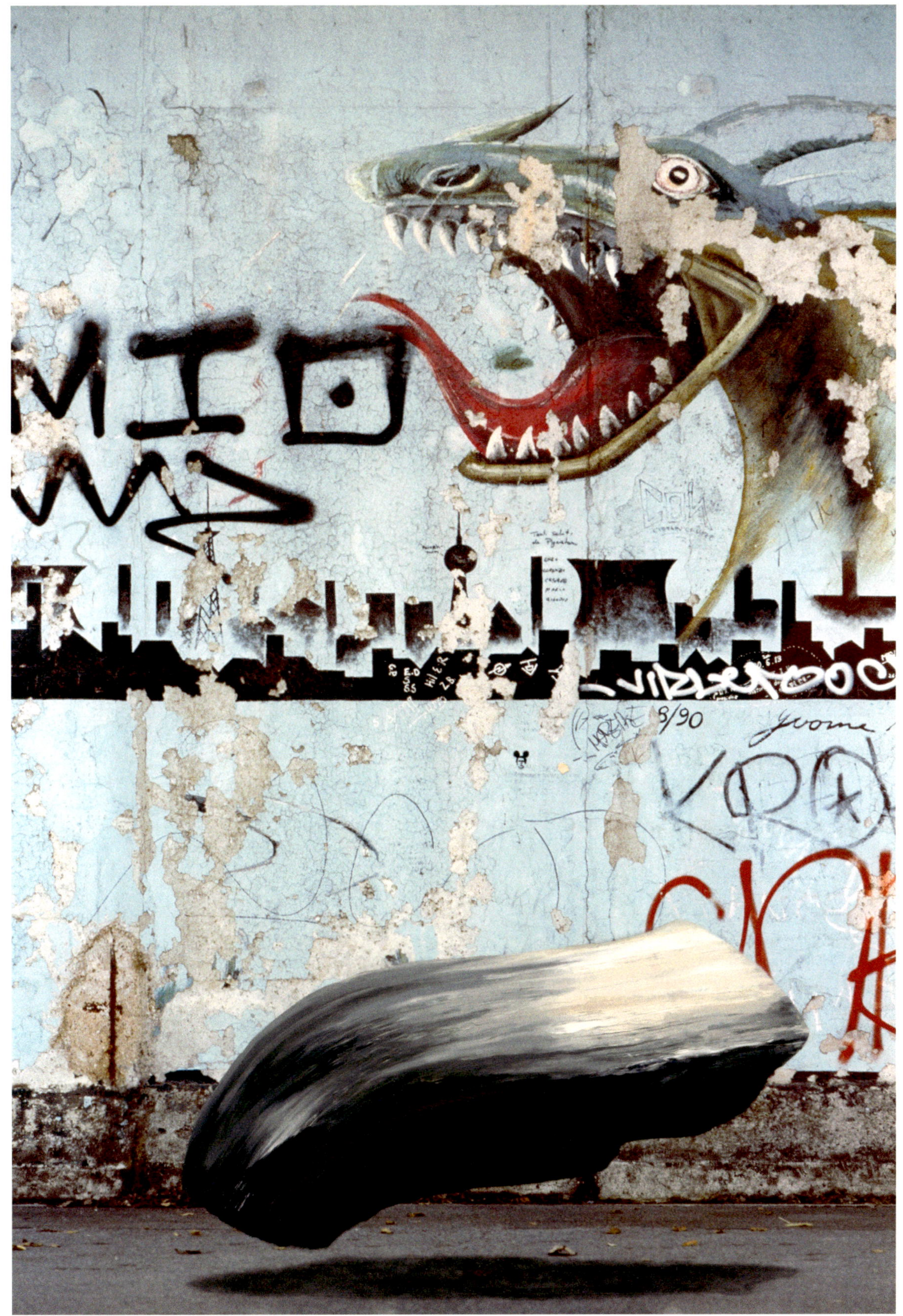

MIO
WAY
8/90
Yvonne

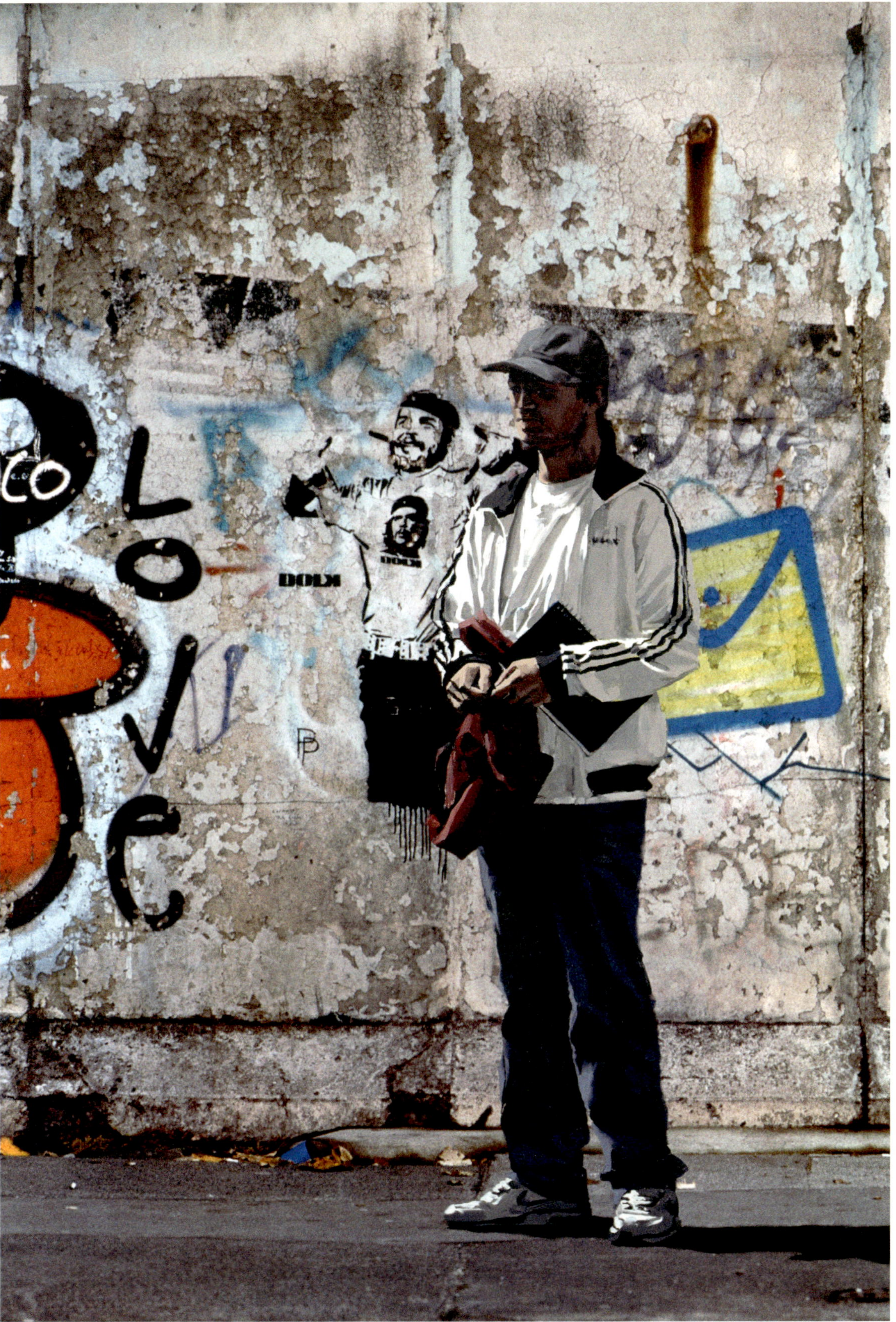

LOVE
CO
DOLK
DOLK

Gemaltes Verschwinden

Zu Marc Lüders

East Side-Serie

Painted Disappearance

On Marc Lüders'

East Side Series

Die Trompe-l'oeil-Malerei täuscht die Augen derartig, dass sie gemalte Gegenstände mit ihren realen Vorbildern verwechseln.

Diese Absicht stand schon hinter dem berühmten antiken Malerwettstreit zwischen Zeuxis und Parrhasios, den letzterer entschied weil er Zeuxis dazu brachte, den gemalten Vorhang vor einem vermeintlichen Gemälde zurückziehen zu wollen. Einer der historischen Höhepunkte des Trompe-l'oeil entwickelte sich als Spezialzweig der Stilllebenmalerei im Holland des 17. Jahrhunderts. Cornelius Gijsbrechts, einer der größten Virtuosen auf diesem Gebiet, stellte neben Vorhängen, geöffneten Fenstern oder Briefablagen auch Rückseiten von Bildern illusionistisch dar.

Seit dem 19. Jahrhundert verlor der malerische Illusionismus zunehmend an Bedeutung, nicht zuletzt durch das Aufkommen der Fotografie. Sie hatte der Malerei die Aufgabe weitgehend abgenommen, die Dinge getreu abzubilden. Doch der Malerei fiel eine neue Aufgabe des Trompe-l'oeil zu, sich selbst in einem anderen Medium vorzutäuschen. Fotos wurden ko-

Trompe-l'oeil painting has traditionally served the function of deceiving the eye to such an extent that painted objects are mistaken for the real depicted objects. This was also the aim of the famous ancient painting contest between Zeuxis and Parrhasios, which the latter won when he succeeded in fooling Zeuxis into wanting to draw back a painted curtain in front of the alleged painting. One of the historic climaxes of trompe-l'oeil developed as a special form of still life painting in Holland in the 17th century. Cornelius Gijsbrechts, one of the greatest virtuosos in this field created illusionary portrayals of curtains, open windows, letter trays, and even the reverse side of pictures.

Since the 19th century, painterly illusionism has become less and less significant, not least due to the development of photography, which to a large extent took over the role of depicting objects true to life. However, painting was assigned a new trompe-l'oeil task; that of simulating itself within another medium. Photographs were coloured and painted to look like paintings in order that they gain recognition as works of art, a

loriert und bemalt, um wie Gemälde aus-
zusehen. Sie sollten dadurch die Anerken-
nung als Kunst erlangen, die rein tech-
nisch hergestellten Lichtbildern lange Zeit
verweigert wurde.

So entwickelte sich im Verhältnis von
Malerei und Fotografie ein merkwürdiger
Nachfolger des klassischen Paragone-
streits, der einst zwischen Malerei und
Skulptur um die »wahrere« Abbildung der
Natur ausgetragen wurde. Gerhard Rich-
ter proklamierte in den 60ger Jahren:

»Alle Maler und überhaupt alle sollten
Fotos abmalen und überall sollten diese
Bilder hängen, in den Wohnungen, den
Gaststätten und Büros, in Bahnhöfen und
Kirchen, also überall.«[1] Neben Richters
malerischer Übertrumpfung fotografischer Unschärfen traten um 1970 die Foto-
realisten mit ihren virtuosen Bildern nach
Fotovorlagen in Erscheinung. Sie brachten
die augentäuscherischen Möglichkeiten
der Malerei noch einmal zu kunsthistori-
schen Ehren, bevor die Möglichkeiten di-
gitaler Bildherstellung und –manipulation
die Frage »Malerei oder Fotografie« in
eine beliebig wählbare Option aus dem
Photoshop-Menü verwandelten.

Künstler treten angesichts neuer Bild-
techniken gern einen Schritt zurück, um
diese besser beobachten zu können. Manet
oder Degas übertrugen die Anschnitte
und Verzerrungen, über die man auf Fotos
gern hinwegsah, in die Malerei, wo der
Rahmen der hier erwarteten Kompositi-
onsregeln sie gleichsam unter ein Vergrö-
ßerungsglas stellte.

status that they were long denied due to
their technical production.

As a result, this position of painting and
photography to one another created an ex-
traordinary successor to the classical
Paragon contest once held between painting and sculpture in the quest for the
»truest« depiction of nature.

In the 60s, Gerhard Richter proclaimed:

»All painters and in fact everyone should
paint from photos and these pictures
should be hung everywhere, in apartments,
in restaurants and offices, in railway sta-
tions and churches, everywhere.«[1] Along-
side Richter's success in taking the blurri-
ness of photography a step further in his
paintings, around 1970 the photo-realists
appeared on the scene, with their virtuoso
pictures created using photographic tem-
plates. They once again gave art-historic
credit to the illusionary possibilities of
painting, before the potential of digital
image production- and manipulation trans-
formed the question »painting or photography« into a random selection of Photo-
shop menu options.

When it comes to new image techniques, artists prefer to take a step back in
order to observe them better. Manet or
Degas transferred the cuts made by the
frame and distortions, which one was in-
clined to overlook in the photos, into their
paintings, where they were quasi magnified
by the anticipated laws of the compositional structure.

And thus it is by no means a sign of historical regression when Marc Lüdgers re-

Und so ist es keineswegs ein historischer Rückschritt, wenn Marc Lüders uns in seinen »Photopicturen« keine Photoshop-Montagen liefert. Er versieht Fotos, die er von realen Landschaften, Brachflächen oder urbanen Situationen gemacht hat, mit einzelnen dazugemalten Elementen.

Scheinbar lässt er die altertümliche Kolorierung und andere Frühformen der fotografischen Täuschung wieder aufleben. Die merkwürdigen, wurstartigen Formen, die auch schon auf Lüders' früheren Schwarzweißbildern herumschwebten, mögen wie Wiedergänger der amorphen Gebilde auf den »Geisterfotografien« Ende des 19. Jahrhunderts wirken. Sie sollten die Existenz übersinnlicher Phänomene beweisen, entpuppten sich aber meist als mehr oder weniger geschickte Fälschungen.

Solche Formen, die manchmal deutlich als Pinselstriche kenntlich sind, manchmal an einen in der Luft schwebenden Klumpen oder Stein erinnern, finden wir auch in Lüders' neuester Bildserie. Sie basiert auf Fotografien die der Künstler an der »East Side Gallery« machte; einem der wenigen übrig gebliebenen Teile der Berliner Mauer, welches 1990 auf 1316 m Länge von über 100 internationalen Künstlern mit meist grellbunten Motiven bemalt wurde.

Bereits der kalte Winter 1990/91 führte zu ersten Schäden an den Bildern, die zwar seit einigen Jahren teilweise restauriert werden, aber immer noch großenteils verwittert, teilweise abgeblättert und

frains from providing Photoshop-collages in his »photopicturen.« Instead, he adds individual painted elements to his photographs of real landscapes, wastelands or urban locations.

It is as if he were to revive the antiquated colouration techniques and other early methods of photographic deception. The curious, sausage-like shapes, which seemed to hover in Lüders' early black-and-white pictures could be perceived as revenants of the amorphic shapes found in the »ghost photographs« at the end of the 19th century. They were intended to prove the existence of supernatural phenomena but frequently revealed themselves to be more or less adept forgeries.

The forms, which are in some cases clearly recognisable as brushstrokes, and which at times resemble blobs or stones hovering in the air, can also be found in Lüders' latest series of pictures. They are based on photographs taken by the artist at the »East Side Gallery»; one of the few remaining sections of the Berlin wall. Here, in 1990 more than 100 international artists painted motifs, mostly in bright colours, along a stretch of 1316 metres.

The succeeding cold winter 1990/91 caused initial damage to the paintings, which, although they have been partially restored in recent years, are still for the most part weathered, and have even flaked off in some sections, or been painted and written over with other graffiti or texts.

Against the background of the photographed sections of the East Side Gallery,

durch andere Graffitis oder Textbotschaften übermalt oder überkritzelt sind.

Vor den fotografierten Abschnitten der East Side Gallery nehmen sich Lüders' malerische »Ergänzungen« wie Bestandteile des bereits auf der Mauer Angebrachten aus. Dass hier eine eigene Realitätsebene vorliegt, wird vor allem durch die gemalten Schatten deutlich, welche die länglichen Striche oder klumpenartigen Formationen auf die Mauer oder auf den Boden zu werfen scheinen. Mit diesem klassischen Trompe-l'oeil-Effekt knüpft Marc Lüders ironisch an den historischen Wettstreit zwischen Malerei und Skulptur an: Der Schatten, klassischer Beweis für die physische Existenz, verleiht dem Gemalten den scheinbaren Realitätsgrad eines im Raum befindlichen Gegenstandes.

Den sich mitunter zu strudelartigen Gebilden auftürmenden, ungegenständlichen Formationen, die in den nummerierten Bildtiteln stets mit »Objekt« klassifiziert sind, steht eine zweite, mit »Figur« bezeichnete Kategorie des »Dazugemalten« gegenüber. Bei diesen Figuren handelt es sich um Menschen, die Lüders zunächst auf öffentlichen Plätzen, an der Ampel stehend oder in anderen beiläufigen Situationen fotografiert hat. Sie tauchten schon in früheren Bilderserien gemalt wieder auf, wo sie einsam im Wald, am Strand oder in einem Gewerbegebiet stehen.

Die Rückenfiguren, die einst von Caspar David Friedrich ähnlich in die Landschaften hineincollagiert wurden, verdoppelten den Blick der Betrachter in die

Lüders' painted »additions« seem to become a part of that which is already written or painted on the wall. The fact that another level of reality is present here is indicated above all by the painted shadows, which the elongated lines or blob-like forms on the wall or on the ground seem to cast. With this classical trompe-l'oeil effect, Marc Lüders makes an ironic reference to the historic battle between painting and sculpture: The shadow, classical proof of physical existence, causes the painted form to appear just as real as an object within a space.

The abstract shapes, which in some cases create swirling structures, and in the numbered titles of the works are always categorized as »objects«, are contrasted by a second category, entitled »figures«, which includes the »painted additions.« These figures are people who Lüders initially photographed in public places, standing at the traffic lights or in other random situations. He also painted these figures in earlier series, standing alone in a wood, on a beach, or in an industrial estate.

The »Rückenfiguren« (back figures), which Caspar David Friedrich once collaged into his landscapes in a similar way, doubled the viewer's gaze into the landscape, which may have been rather dreamy, but was in fact directed quite purposely into the distance. Lüders' figures are also frequently shown from behind. However, even when they are positioned sideways or frontally, their gaze is not directed at the viewer. Their faces are not clearly recognizable and they stand about

Landschaft, der zwar verträumt sein mag, aber doch einigermaßen zielgerichtet nach hinten geht. Auch Lüders' Figuren sieht man häufig von hinten. Doch wenn sie seitlich oder frontal stehen, geht der Blick nicht in Richtung Betrachter. Ihre Gesichter sind nie deutlich zu erkennen und sie stehen beziehungslos wie orientierungslose Fremde in der »neuen« Umgebung herum.

Vielleicht ist es nicht übertrieben darin auch eine Metapher für die Beiläufigkeit der Beziehungen zwischen den Menschen in der Großstadt zu sehen, wie sie schon von Edgar Allan Poe, Baudelaire oder dem deutschen Soziologen Georg Simmel eindringlich beschrieben wurde. Auf vielen Fotografien urbaner Milieus findet sich ein Eindruck mentaler Abwesenheit wie eine Signatur des modernen Lebens, etwa in den »Subway Portraits«, die Walker Evans zwischen 1938 und 1940 mit versteckter Kamera von Passagieren in der New Yorker U-Bahn machte.

Ähnlich wie Evans nimmt Lüders Passanten auf, deren Nicht-Wissen um das Fotografiertwerden sie mental abwesend erscheinen lassen. In der East Side-Serie findet sich einerseits kein Bezug der Figuren zu uns als Betrachter, andererseits lassen sie kaum eine Aufmerksamkeit zum Hintergrund der bemalten Mauer erkennen.

Der Bezug von Figur und Hintergrund ist ein kompositorischer, den Lüders durch die Platzierung der Figur im Bild und durch die Farben von Kleidung, Ta-

in their »new« surroundings like disoriented strangers.

It is perhaps no exaggeration to perceive this as a metaphor for the random nature of the relationships between people in large cities, such as Edgar Allan Poe, Baudelaire, or the German sociologist Georg Simmel once vividly described them. An impression of mental absence can be found in many photographs of urban milieus, like a signature of modern life, for example in the »Subway Portraits«, photographs of passengers in the New York metro shot by Walker Evans between 1938 and 1940 using a hidden camera.

In a similar manner to Evans, Lüders photographs passers-by who, oblivious of this fact, also seem mentally absent. In the East Side series, the figures do not strive to relate to us as viewers, nor do they seem to pay any attention to the painted wall behind them.

The relationship between the figure and the background is of a compositional nature, created by Lüders' positioning of the figure in the picture and by his choice of colours for the clothing, bags or other accessories. Similarities in the colours and forms create a compositional uniformity.

And the more colourfully the persons are dressed, the better they can be »concealed« in their surroundings. Someone who wants to remain invisible in the countryside or in a wood is more likely to choose dark or subdued camouflage colours or patterns similar to foliage, such as is used in traditional military camouflage clothing.

schen oder anderer Accessoires herstellt. Farbliche und formale Korrespondenzen stellen eine kompositorische Vereinheitlichung her.

Und je bunter die Personen gekleidet sind, desto besser sind sie in der Umgebung »versteckt«. Wer in einer Landschaft, in einem Wald unsichtbar bleiben will, wird eher dunkle und zurückhaltende Tarnfarben oder laubfarbene Musterungen wählen, wie sie die traditionelle militärische Tarnkleidung aufweist.

Als 1915 Kanonen mit Camouflage-Bemalung durch Paris fuhren, soll Picasso zu Gertrude Stein gesagt haben: »Das haben wir erfunden.«[2]

Tatsächlich gibt es viel Vergleichbares zwischen der kubistischen Formzerlegung mit der Picasso und Braque die traditionellen Objektbeziehungen in ein zersplittertes Mosaik aus Einzelformen auflösten und militärischen Tarnbemalungen, die einen Gegenstand in seiner Umgebung optisch zum Verschwinden bringen sollen.

So gesehen scheint es geradezu folgerichtig, dass William Wadsworth und andere Vertreter des Vortizismus, der britischen Spielart des Kubismus, gegen Ende des Ersten Weltkriegs mit der Beaufsichtigung des Tarnanstriches von 2000 Schiffen beauftragt wurden.

Auch die East Side Gallery ist eine Art Camouflage-Bemalung: Sie sollte das triste Grau der Betonplatten verbergen, wie schon die zahlreichen Graffitis, die vor 1990 die Westseite der Berliner Mauer geziert hatten.

When in 1915 canons painted with camouflage were driven through Paris, Picasso allegedly said to Gertrude Stein: »We invented that.«[2]

And in fact there are many similarities between the Cubistic dissection of form with which Picasso and Braque dissolved the traditional relationships between objects in order to create a fragmentary mosaic of individual shapes, and military camouflage paintings, which aim to make an object vanish within its surroundings.

In view of this it would seem quite logical that William Wadsworth and other representatives of Vorticism, a British variety of Cubism, were given the task of overseeing the camouflage painting of 2000 ships towards the end of the First World War.

The East Side Gallery is also a kind of camouflage painting: its goal was to disguise the drab grey of the concrete slabs, just like the numerous examples of graffiti that had adorned the west side of the Berlin wall prior to 1990.

The fact that the »East Side«, once part of the wall in the former border section sheltering East Berlin from view from the west, was also painted with graffiti and other images, was perceived as a conscious and liberating comment on the political changes, and was reflected in the content of the individual graffiti artworks.

The effects of weathering and the constant painting over of the pictures transform the former clear messages into a complex jumble of colours, shapes, texts, and symbols. These would certainly have

Dass auch die »East Side«, ein einst den Grenzbereich nach Ostberlin hin abschirmender Mauerabschnitt, nach der Maueröffnung mit Graffitis und anderen Bildern bemalt wurde, verstand sich als bewusster und befreiender Kommentar zu den politischen Veränderungen, die in den einzelnen Werken der Graffitikünstler inhaltlich reflektiert wurden.

Die Verwitterungen und Übermalungen machen aus den ehemals klaren Botschaften ein komplexes Wirrwarr aus Farben, Formen, Texten und Zeichen. Sie hätten sicher Fotografen wie Brassaï fasziniert, der schon in den 1930er Jahren Graffitis oder abgerissene Plakate aufnahm und damit die pittoreske Verfallsästhetik modernisierte, die schon im 19. Jahrhundert den Geschmack vieler Fotografen an Ruinen und verfallenden und verwitterten Mauerflächen entzündete. Was Brassaï noch in grafischem Schwarzweiß einfing, hängten die »Plakatabreisser« wie Raymond Hains oder Jacques de la Villeglé um 1960 als vielfarbige Bildobjekte ins Museum. Schon ihre Bilder gäben eine gute Tarnumgebung ab, vor der die Figuren von Lüders in ihrer poppig-bunten Straßenkleidung, ihren T-Shirts mit Logos oder Schriftzügen optisch nahezu verschwinden würden.

Um das Gegenteil geht es den Touristen, die sich vor der realen East Side Gallery, auf dem Bürgersteig entlang der vielbefahrenen Mühlenstraße zwischen Ostbahnhof und Oberbaumbrücke von ihren Verwandten oder Freunden ablichten lassen. Sie wollen zeigen, dass sie hier

interested photographers such as Brassaï, who back in the 1930s integrated graffiti or torn posters into his works, thus modernising the picturesque aesthetic of decay, which in the 19th century had already sparked off the interest of many photographers in ruins and in derelict and weatherbeaten walls. Affichistes such as Raymond Hains or Jacques de la Villeglé took what Brassaï captured in graphic black-and-white, and hung it as polychrome visual objects in museums around 1960. Their pictures would provide a good camouflage background against which Lüders' figures would virtually disappear in their brightly-coloured streetwear and their T-shirts adorned with logos or text.

The opposite applies to the tourists, photographed by their friends or relatives in front of the real East Side Gallery, on the pavement along the busy Mühlenstraße between Ostbahnhof and Oberbaumbrücke. They want to show that they were here, something that was probably never the case with the people in Lüders' pictures.

The latter have been collaged with paint into surroundings that are already a collage, one that has built up diverse layers on a remaining section of the Berlin wall over the past eighteen years.

Even if no-one could possibly succeed in determining the origins and creators of all the pictures and symbols left behind, these are traces that can be perceived physically. Marc Lüders, who in earlier works also added painted graffiti to photographed walls, adds carefully selected elements,

waren, was bei den Personen auf Lüders' Bildern wahrscheinlich nie der Fall war.

Sie sind malerisch hineincollagiert in eine Umgebung, die bereits eine Collage ist, die sich im Laufe der letzten achtzehn Jahre in diversen Schichten auf einem Rest der Berliner Mauer abgelagert hat.

Auch wenn niemand in der Lage sein dürfte, Herkunft und Urheber all der hinterlassenen Bilder und Zeichen zu ermitteln, handelt es sich um physisch erfahrbare Spuren. Ihnen hat Marc Lüders, der schon in einigen früheren Bildern fotografierte Wände mit gemalten Graffitis versah, gezielt Elemente hinzufügt, die zu einer manchmal reliefartig erhabenen physischen Spur auf der Oberfläche des Fotos werden. Die abstrakten Formen, die manchmal wie ein spontan gesetzter Pinselstrich aussehen, sind eher Zeichen für die Spontaneität der malerischen Geste als wirklich spontan. Man könnte sie als illusionistische Darstellung eines gestischen Pinselhiebs verstehen, als gemaltes Trompe-l'oeil der Malerei selbst.

Und damit wären wir doch bei einem ganz anderen Thema als dem Wettstreit zwischen Fotografie und Malerei, den Marc Lüders nur scheinbar noch einmal aufführt, um der Nivellierung aller Medien durch ihre digitale Simulation ein kleines analoges Schnippchen zu schlagen. Lüders fotografiert, was gemalt ist, malt selbst etwas dazu, und dieses Gemalte wirft einen Schatten in der realen Umgebung. Das Einzige, dessen »Realität« wir physisch überprüfen können, ist die Erha-

which sometimes become relief-like, tangible, physical traces on the surface of the photos. The abstract shapes, which at times resemble spontaneous brushstrokes, are not really spontaneous, but are rather symbolic of the spontaneity of painterly gestures. One could interpret them as the illusionary depiction of a gestural brushstroke, a painted trompe-l'oeil of painting itself.

And that would lead us to quite a different theme, away from the battle between photography and painting, which Marc Lüders appears to re-enact only to once again analogically outwit the levelling of all mediums by means of their digital simulation. Lüders photographs what has been painted, paints something more, and this painted addition then casts a shadow in its real surroundings. The only case where »reality« can really be physically examined is when it comes to the sublime nature of painting. If we take the physical reality as a starting point, which is visible in the photo the work is based on, then the painted elements suggest an added layer with a lesser degree of reality. Different levels of visual representation are engaged in play with one another, which constantly questions their lack of ambiguity. The alleged interplay of painting and photography is rather a staged performance of that which quasi takes place behind the curtain of the screen, in the case of digitally-generated pictures. If painting, photography and other digital visual media only compete when simulated, then there are no longer

benheit der Malerei. Von der physischen Realität ausgehend, die auf dem zugrunde liegenden Foto zu sehen ist, suggerieren die gemalten Elemente eine hinzugefügte Ebene von geringerem Realitätsgrad. Verschiedene Ebenen der visuellen Darstellung werden in ein Spiel miteinander verwickelt, das ihre Eindeutigkeit immer wieder in Frage stellt. Das vermeintliche Wechselspiel zwischen Malerei und Fotografie ist eher eine szenische Aufführung dessen, was sich bei digital generierten Bildern gleichsam hinter dem Vorhang der Bildschirmoberfläche vollzieht. Wenn Malerei, Fotografie und andere Bildmedien nur noch simuliert gegeneinander antreten, gibt es keine physischen Spuren mehr, deren Realität in Frage zu stellen wäre. Und damit entfällt auch die notwendige Reibungsfläche für das illusionistische Spiel des Trompe-l'oeil, das Marc Lüders ebenso raffiniert wie zeitgemäß am Leben zu erhalten weiß.

von: Ludwig Seyfarth

any physical traces whose reality could be called into question. And with that, the source of friction required for the illusionary game of trompe-l'oeil, which Marc Lüders keeps alive in a manner that is both contemporary and ingenious, can be disposed of

text: Ludwig Seyfarth, February 2008
translation: Gillian Morris

---

1. Gerhard Richter, Text für Ausstellungskatalog der Galerie h, Hannover, zusammen mit Sigmar Polke [1966], in: ders., Text. Schriften und Interviews, hg. von Hans-Ulrich Obrist, Frankfurt a. M./Leipzig 1996, S. 42.

2. siehe dazu und zum Folgenden: Christoph Asendorf, Super Constellation – Flugzeug und Raumrevolution, Wien/New York 1997, S. 217 f.

1. Gerhard Richter, text for exhibition catalogue for the Galerie h, Hannover, together with Sigmar Polke [1966], in: idem., Text. Schriften und Interviews, published by Hans-Ulrich Obrist, Frankfurt a. M./Leipzig1996, p. 42.

2. See also: Christoph Asendorf, Super Constellation – Flugzeug und Raumrevolution, Vienna/New York 1997, p. 217 f.

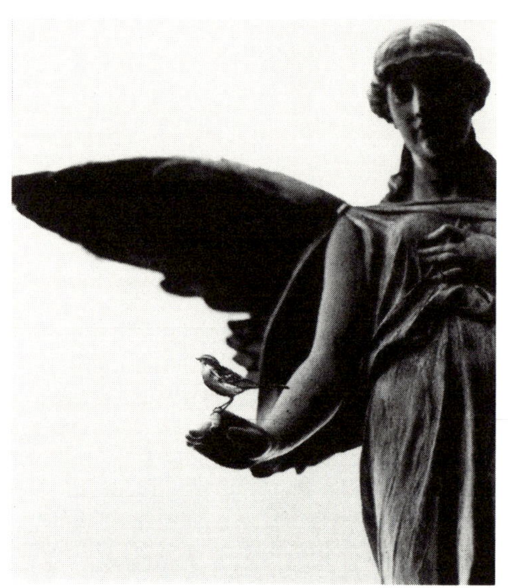

Vogel 507-1-2, Öl auf Silbergelatine-Print , 72 x 60 cm, 2001

MARC LÜDERS:
Das Schemenhafte im Sucher eines Existenzialisten

MARC LÜDERS:
An Existentialist's Take On The Uncanny

Heute glaubt niemand mehr an eine tiefere »Wahrheit« der Fotografie oder an ihre Fähigkeit, Realität objektiv darzustellen. Zumindest niemand in der Welt der Kunst. Solche Begriffe sind längst durch Künstler wie Joseph Kosuth, Sherrie Levine, Cindy Sherman und Gerhard Richter entzaubert worden. Es überrascht nicht, dass der Fotograf von heute immer öfter auf Inszenierungen oder digital erweiterte Bilder zurückgreift, deren Manipulationen das Fotografische offen als Konstrukt und Fiktion deklarieren.

Selbst wenn die Zukunft der Fotografie besiegelt scheint, ihr Einfluss auf unser Leben ist es noch lange nicht. So viel fotobasiertes Bild war nie, vom Einfluss inoffizieller Videos auf die US-Präsidentenwahlen 2008 bis hin zu Phänomenen wie dem Handy-Dating in Japan. Wir alle sind Junkies dieser Bildzitate, ohne die wir in der aktuellen Konsumwelt nicht mehr überlebensfähig wären, ohne die auch unser eigenes Schicksal besiegelt wäre. Sie sind die Lingua franca unseres globalen Zeitalters, das, was Henri Cartier-Bresson den »entscheidenden Moment« nannte, und

No one really believes in the essential »truth« of photography anymore, or in its capacity to represent objective reality. At least nobody in the art world. Such notions were dismantled long ago by artists like Joseph Kosuth, Sherrie Levine, Cindy Sherman, and Gerhard Richter, among others. Its no surprise then that the trend in photography these days favors the set-up or digitally enhanced model, where manipulation overtly expresses the idea of the photograph as a construct or fiction.

Still, if photography's bias has become a foregone conclusion, its role in our lives is everything but. From the impact of »viral« videos on the 2008 U.S. Presidential elections to the phenomena of cell phone dating in Japan, the proliferation of photo-based images is unprecedented, as is our dependence on them. We are all addicted to the visual sound bite, without which we - as viable citizens in this consumer culture - can consider ourselves foregone conclusions. It is the lingua franca of our global age, what Henri Cartier-Bresson famously deemed »the decisive moment,« and it all hinges on photography's promise of instantaneity.

alles hängt am Versprechen der Fotografie auf Unmittelbarkeit.

Wie ironisch, dass wir uns immer mehr auf fotografische Bilder verlassen und umgekehrt immer weniger an ihre Wahrheit glauben. Dies ist kein geringes Dilemma für zeitgenössische Künstler, insbesondere für solche, die mit Fotomaterial arbeiten. Es stellt sie vor eine fast unlösbare Aufgabe: ein Bild zu schaffen, das den Blick des Betrachters hält, ohne dass sie dabei auf aufwendige Tableaus oder Tohuwabohu-Taktiken zurückgreifen müssten. Genau das macht die fotobasierte Arbeit von Marc Lüders so faszinierend. Seine hybriden Bilder aus gemalten Figuren und abstrakten Objekten auf Fotografien von Stadt-, Architektur-, Innenraum- und Naturlandschaften vermitteln keine plausible Wahrheit oder augenfällige Geschichte und beruhen auch nicht auf technischen Tricks. Und doch bleiben diese sanften Bilddichotomien im Gedächtnis des Betrachters haften, sie graben sich ein wie hingehauchte Rätsel.

Wenn wir den auf der Hand eines Grabengels gelandeten Vogel lange genug betrachten (*Vogel 507-1-2, 2001*) und dann merken, dass er gemalt ist und nicht »echt«, oder die junge Frau ansehen, die allein in einem abgelegenen Industriepark steht und hilflos auf den Boden starrt (*Figur 613-8-5, 2004*), erfasst uns plötzlich ein Schauder. Wir merken, wie wir selbst mitten in Lüders' wabernder Realität gelandet sind, und suchen sie in nachdenklicher Isolierung zu ergründen. Was ist echt

How ironic then that our reliance on the photographic image seems only to grow in direct relation to our distrust in its truth. It is quite a predicament for contemporary artists, particularly those engaged in a photo-based practice. It sets up a nearly impossible task: the creation of an image that can sustain a viewer's attention without resorting to elaborate tableaux or razzle-dazzle tactics. This is what makes the photo-based work of Marc Lüders so intriguing. His hybrid images of painted figures and abstract blurs on photographs of landscape (urban, architectural, domestic, and natural) evidence no plausible truth, obvious narrative, or technical tricks. Yet these quietly disjunctive works insinuate themselves in the mind of the viewer, burrowing in like the vaguest of riddles.

If we look long enough at the bird perched on the hand of a funerary angel in *Vogel 507-1-2*, 2001, and discover that it's painted, and not »real,« or wonder at the young woman who stands alone in a remote industrial park, gazing forlornly at the ground (*Figur 613-8-5*, 2004), their perplexing mystery draws us in. We too find ourselves perching on Lüders' errant reality, pondering it in pensive isolation. What's real and what's not? they ask. And is photography any more relevant in this respect than painting? More importantly, do these questions have the same meaning in a virtual world?

Lüders' work in this sense can be best described as an existentialist take on the

und was nicht?, fragen sie uns. Ist hier nun die Fotografie relevanter oder die Malerei? Mehr noch: Haben diese Fragen in einer virtuellen Welt dieselbe Bedeutung?

Die Arbeit von Lüders kann in diesem Sinne am besten als ein existenzialistischer Zugriff auf das Schemenhafte beschrieben werden. Gerade indem er die Priorität des Fotoabzugs und seiner befrachteten Geschichte betont, gelingt es ihm durch seine gemalten »Eingriffe«, beide zu entmachten. Sie stellen das in Frage, was wir zu sehen und zu wissen meinen, um herauszustreichen, dass das am Wichtigsten ist, was wir auch glauben wollen. Und Lüders zielt mit seinen »veränderten Wahrheiten« genau darauf hin: So verleiht er seinen abstrakten Objekten Schatten, die durch die Schwarzweißaufnahmen leerer Badezimmer und barocker Säle schweben und uns von deren Präsenz überzeugen sollen. Denn Lüders glaubt als Künstler ganz fest an die Logik der Vorstellung und die Kraft der Illusion.

Lüders' jüngste Werkreihe *East Side Gallery* bildet darin keine Ausnahme. Die Schichtung von Darstellung über Darstellung hinterfragt das Wesen der Wahrnehmung, aber auch die Rolle des Glaubens an Bilder in unserem Informationszeitalter. Darüber hinaus widersetzen sich die Werke einfachen Antworten, ihre veränderten Wahrheiten werfen Fragen auf, die gerade sehr aktuell sind. Dass diese Bilder nun nicht wie ihre Vorgänger »aussehen« (wenn auch unbeabsichtigt), erwischt uns erneut auf dem falschen

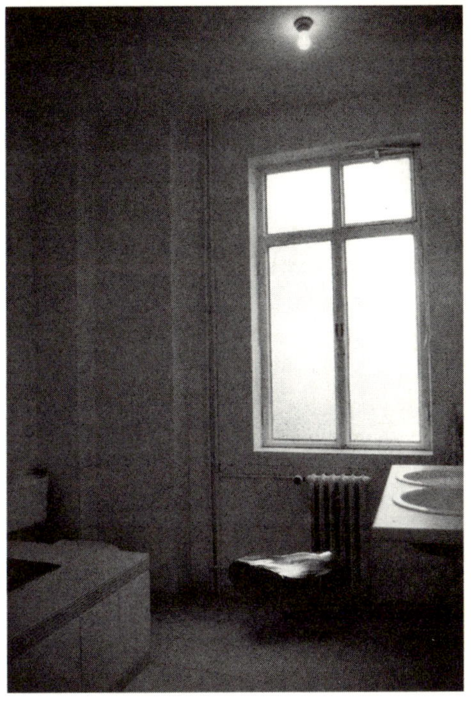

uncanny. By underscoring the primacy of the photographic image and its freighted history, his painted »interventions« effectively disable both. They challenge what we think we see, and what we think we know in order to point out that what choose to believe is really what matters most. And Lüders calculates his »altered truths« to just this end, adding shadows, for example, to the abstract blurs that flit through his black-and-white photographs of empty bathrooms and bygone parlors to convince us of their presence. For as an artist, Luders believes in the logic of the imagination, and the power of illusion.

Objekt 381-4-3, Öl auf Silbergelatine-Print, 40 x 30 cm, 1999

Bein und enttäuscht unsere Erwartungen schon wieder.

Wie alle seine Serien begann auch *East Side Gallery* damit, dass der Künstler für seine gemalten Mise-en-scènes zunächst ein besonderes Setting fotografierte. In der Vergangenheit war dies stets ein nüchterner, bestenfalls atmosphärischer Hintergrund, und nun hat er dafür zum ersten Mal ein bedeutendes Symbol der deutschen Zeitgeschichte gewählt: die Berliner Mauer.

Obgleich die soziopolitischen Implikationen eines solchen Symbols nicht ignoriert werden können, hält Lüders fest, »dass der politische Aspekt nicht mein Hauptanliegen war. Als ich die letzten noch stehenden Überreste der Berliner Mauer das erste Mal sah, mit all den Graffiti, war ich fasziniert von der Idee, auf Malerei zu malen, auf etwas, das in der Öffentlichkeit durch verschiedene Personen entstanden ist. Diese Menschen sind aus allen Teilen der Welt angereist, um ein historisches Bauwerk zu sehen, das für die Trennung zweier Systeme steht. Was sie aber sehen, ist eine lange Aneinanderreihung von Bildern. Und sie nehmen selbst Teil an der Entstehung und Veränderung dieser Malerei auf der Mauer, indem sie ihre Namen dazuschreiben und damit ihre Anwesenheit dokumentieren. Auf diese Weise verwandelt sich die Mauer in eine riesige Leinwand.«

Und zu einem endlosen Work-in-progress, möchte man hinzufügen, angesichts dessen man – wie beim Zeitlauf der Ge-

Lüders' latest body of work, *East Side Gallery*, is no exception. Its layering of representation upon representation also questions the nature of perception, and the role of faith in relation to images in this information age. Moreover, they too defy easy answers, submitting their altered truths as

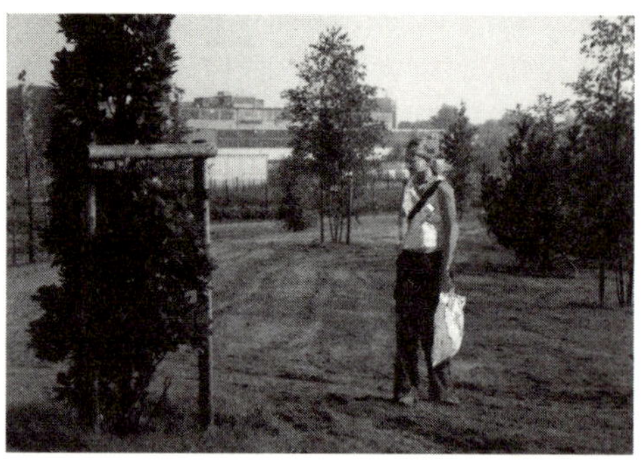

questions that bear new consideration. That the images »look« unlike any of his previous works, however unintentionally, further catches us off guard, disrupting our expectations once again.

Like all his series, *East Side Gallery* began with the artist selecting and photographing a particular setting for his painted mise-en-scènes. In the past, it's always been something mundane or atmospheric, but for the first time ever, Lüders has chosen a highly charged symbol of the contemporary German landscape: the Berlin Wall.

Yet while the sociopolitical implications of such a symbol are impossible to ignore, Lüders maintains »the political aspect was

Figur 613-8-5, Öl auf C-Print, 12 x 17 cm, 2003

schichte oder der Entwicklung des Ich – wählen kann, ob man lediglich Zeuge sein oder seine eigenen Spuren hinterlassen will. Keineswegs überraschend ist, dass sich Lüders für beides entschließt und die zwei Akte in einen zusammenlegt. Dokumentarischer Wille und kreativer Ausdruck verschmelzen zu denselben unfasslich-schlüpfrigen Objekten wie die Fotografie-Malerei-Hybride, deren Teil sie sind.

Wenn er seine einsamen Gestalten und Objekte vor die graffiti-besprayten Reste der Berliner Mauer stellt, dann verfährt Lüders bei den abstrakten Farbstreifen mit größerer Sorgfalt als in vergangenen Arbeiten. Mit so großer, dass sie schließlich »realer« erscheinen als ihr fotografischer Hintergrund, welcher seinerseits wiederum mehr Malerei enthält. Und obwohl die quasivergrößerten Pinselstriche genau so viel Gestus vermitteln wie zuvor, haben sie menschliche Maße erhalten, so dass sie gewichtiger erscheinen – sowohl im wörtlichen als auch übertragenen Sinn. Die Abmessungen der Color Prints sind mit 160 x 106 cm auch wesentlich größer als die von Lüders in der Vergangenheit verwendeten, wodurch beide Techniken noch einmal mehr (illusorische) Wirkung entfalten. Wenn der schmale Streifen asphaltierten Gehsteigs nicht wäre, der das aufgemalte Objekt in fast allen dieser Bilder von der bemalten Mauer räumlich trennt, wäre die fotografische Tiefe nur schwer zu erkennen – und damit der nie ganz verschwindende Hinweis, wo Lüders' Eingriffe beginnen und enden. Wenn auch die Figuren

not my chief interest. When I first saw the remaining fragments of the Berlin Wall, and all the graffiti it has, I was fascinated by the prospect of painting on a painting; something created in public by people from all over the world. People who came to see a historical building representing the separation of two systems, and encountered an onslaught of pictures, which they in turn took part in by adding their own 'mark'. The wall has become a giant canvas.«

And a perpetual work-in-progress, one might add, in the face of which - like the march of history or the evolution of »I« - one can elect to merely witness, or add their own mark. Not surprisingly Lüders chooses both, conflating the two acts as one. Documentary impulse and creative expression merge with the same slippery blur as the photography-painting hybrids they represent.

Rendering the same solitary figures and swaths of abstract paint over graffitied sections of the Berlin Wall, Lüders paints the former with greater refinement than in past works. So much they appear more »real« than their photographic backdrops, which by turn are more painterly in contrast. And though the abstract strokes are as gestural as ever, they are given a human scale, making them weightier - literally and conceptually - in the process. The size of these color prints at 160 x 106 centimeters (or 3.5 x 5.2 feet, approximately) is also significantly larger than what Lüders used in the past, the results exaggerating again the illusory effects of both. If it weren't for the small

in ihrer Camouflage die visuellen Bruch-
stellen früherer Werke vermissen lassen,
das Geheimnis hinter diesen Bildern ist
keinesfalls weniger anspielungsreich.

Nehmen wir etwa *733-10-1, 2007* (S. 35),
worin ein junger Mann in weißen Hemdsär-
meln und dunkler Hose steht, im Profil
leicht zur Mauer gedreht. Wegen der ver-
borgenen Hände und des im Schatten liegenden Gesichts ist seine Stimmung trotz
des hellen Tageslichts nicht erkennbar. Ist
er ein Einheimischer in der Mittagspause,
der stehen bleibt, um auf der Mauer, die er
so gut kennt, einen neu angebrachten
Schriftzug zu studieren? Oder ist er ein
Künstler auf der Durchreise, der eben eine
Vorlesung über Kunst im öffentlichen
Raum gehalten hat und nach einem »Tag«
eines legendären Sprayers sucht? Wer
weiß? Auch für Lüders mag das im Dun-
keln liegen, und seine Positionierung der
Figur (einem anderen fotografischen
Schauplatz entlehnt) vor diesem Mauerabschnitt mag genauso eine formale Ent-
scheidung gewesen sein wie alles andere.
Der schwarze Kreis um das gesprayte
»MARIA 2005 SPAIN« und der hellgraue
Bogen eines schwarz berandeten Fett-
schriftbuchstabens umklammern den jun-
gen Mann in einer visuellen Dynamik miteinander kommunizierender Linien. Auch
in *733-3-2, 2007* (S. 77) ist eine sorgfältige
Repetition von Form, Farbe und Linien-
führung zu erkennen: im Hintergrund das
vertikale Mauer-Diptychon oder -Tripty-
chon mit der futuristischen Skyline und
dem riesigen Drachen im oberen Bereich,

strip of cemented sidewalk that spatially
separates the painted image · from the
painted wall in nearly all these images; the
photographic presence would be difficult
to detect; evidence of where Lüders' interventions begin and end, all but disappear-
ing. But while the figures lack the visual dis-
cord of earlier works in their camouflage
effect, the mystery of the images is no less
insinuating.

Consider *Figur 733-10-1*, 2007, (page 35)
in which a young man stands in white shirt-
sleeves and black pants, profile slightly
turned toward the wall behind him. Hands
hidden, face in shadow, his emotional state
is indecipherable despite the bright light of
day. Is he a local on a lunch break, stopping
to study a new graphic scrawled on the wall
that he knows so well? Or is he a visiting
artist who's just given a lecture on public
art, and wants to find a famous tag by
some legendary activist. Who knows? Even
Lüders may be in the dark, his positioning
of this figure (displaced from another photographic locale) on this section of the wall
as much a formal decision as anything else.
The black swirl of »Maria 2005 Spain« and
the whitish-gray curl of a bubble letter out-
lined in black frame the young man in a visual dynamic of echoing lines. *Objekt 733-
3-2*, 2007 (page 77) also reveals the careful
repetition of shape, color, and line. In it, a
vertical diptych features a futuristic skyline
and giant dragon in the top register, and
one of Lüders signature blurbs floating just
above the sidewalk, midway up the bottom
register. The slight S-shaped curve of the

während in der unteren Bildhälfte eines dieser Lüdersschen Markenzeichen über dem Bürgersteig schwebt. Die sförmige Kurve des schwarzweißen Objekt-Signets, das in seinen eigenen Schatten zu fallen scheint, spiegelt die herausgestreckte rote Zunge des Drachens und bildet in Größe und schwerer schwarzer Form ein perfektes Gegenstück zum darüber brüllenden Drachen.

Alle von Lüders' Bildern verbinden ästhetische Fertigkeit mit konzeptuellem Scharfsinn und beweisen damit, dass Schönheit und Intellekt nicht gegensätzlicher sind als irgendeine der anderen Unterscheidungen, die er so spielerisch aufhebt, wie etwa diejenige zwischen Fotografie und Malerei, zwischen Wahrheit und Fiktion, zwischen Realität und Illusion. In Lüders' existentialistischer Sichtweise ist alles eine Sache der Wahrnehmung. Wie Nietzsche, der an berühmter Stelle sagt, Plato sei langweilig, sieht auch Lüders die Realität als ein kontingentes, offenes Spiel von Zeichen. Die Sichtweise, Kunst sei nichts anderes als eine Nachahmung der Natur, weist er damit weit von sich und stellt so den Begriff der Mimesis selbst auf den Kopf. Mit der Logik der Vorstellung und der Kraft der Illusion feiert sein Werk das Irrationale und macht letztlich aus uns allen Gläubige.

black-and white blurb, which seems to gravitate toward its shadow on the ground, mirrors in reverse the dragon's lashing red tongue; its scale and heavy black form in perfect counterbalance to the looming dragon above.

Of course, all of Lüders images marry aesthetic skill with conceptual acumen, proving that beauty and intellect are no less opposed than any of the other divisions he manifestly dissolves such as that of photography and painting; truth and fiction; reality and illusion. Everything is contingent on perception in Lüders existentialist vision. Like Nietzsche, who famously proclaimed, »Plato was a bore,« Lüders also regards nature/reality as a contingent, open play of signs, not some absolute truth to be governed by reason. As such he dismisses the very prospect of art as imitation, turning Plato's notion of mimesis on its head. Through the logic of the imagination and the power of illusion, his work celebrates the irrational, and in the end, makes believers of us all.

Jane Ursula Harris, February 2008

Jane Ursula Harris, Februar 2008
Aus dem Englischen von Andreas Münzner

Biografie

1963	**geboren in Hamburg**
1984	**Ausbildung zum Buchhändler**
1986	**Fachhochschule für Gestaltung, Hamburg**
1994	**Studium Anthropologie und Philosophie an der**
	Johannes Gutenberg - Universität Mainz
1997	**Arbeitsstipendium der Stadt Hamburg**
2002	**Stipendium der Deutschen Akademie Rom,**
	Villa Massimo für die Casa Baldi in Olevano Romano
Seit 2005	**Lehrauftrag für Malerei im Fachbereich Gestaltung**
	an der Hochschule für Angewandte Wissenschaften (HAW) in Hamburg

Biography

1963	born in Hamburg
1984	trained as book-seller
1986	studied at Hamburg University of Applied Sciences
1994	studied at Johanes Gutenberg-University Mainz
	anthropology and philosophy
1997	scholarship of the city of Hamburg
2002	scholarship of the German academy Rome
	Villa Massimo for Casa Baldi in Olevano Romano Italy
Since 2005	teaching assignment »painting«
	at the Hamburg University of Applied Sciences

Sammlungen **Werke von Lüders befinden sich u.a. im Museum of Contemporary Photography Chicago, Nord/LB, Hannover, DZ Bank Frankfurt am Main und in vielen europäischen und us-amerikanischen Privatsammlungen.**

Collections Works of Lüders are in the following collections: Museum of Contemporary Photography Chicago, Nord/LB, Hannover, DZ Bank Frankfurt am Main and in several private collections in Europe and the USA.

Ausstellungen (Auswahl)

2008   *East Side Gallery*, Galerie Levy, Hamburg und pablo's birthday,
New York (E), Katalog

2007   *Displaced Persons*, pablo's birthday, New York (E)
Marc Lüders - Photopicturen, Haus der Kunst, Brünn (E)
Zwischen Konstruktion und Reduktion, Sammlung Hupertz, Stiftung Schleswig-
Holsteinische Landesmuseen Schloß Gottorf, Schleswig (G), Katalog
SCHÖNWAHNSINNIG, Sammlung CC, Stiftung Schleswig-Holsteinische
Landesmuseen Schloss Gottorf, Schleswig (G), Katalog

2006   *In Flagranti II*, Dortmunder Kunstverein (G), Katalog
Vier Positionen zum Thema Landschaft, Galerie Kamolz, Braunschweig (G)
Four German Artists, Sara Tecchia Gallery, New York (G)

2005   *Marc Lüders*, Artgalerie7, Köln (E)
Painting on Photography - Photography on Painting, Museum of Contemporary
Photography, Chicago (G)
Marc Lüders, Wilhem-Hack-Museum, Rudolf-Scharpf-Galerie, Ludwigshafen (E)
Marc Lüders - Neue Photopicturen, Galerie Levy, Hamburg (E)
Marc Lüders, pablo's birthday, New York (E)
Galerie im Prater und Galerie Walden, Berlin (G)

2004   *Marc Lüders*, Galerie Terminus, München (E)
Marc Lüders – Bildrealitäten, NORD/LB art gallery, Hannover (E), Katalog
Der Mediale Blick des Malers II »Marc Lüders – Photopicturen«,
Galerie im Park, Bremen (E)

2003   *Marc Lüders - Photopicturen*, Galerie Levy, Hamburg (E), Katalog
*Der Augenblick ist Ewigkeit – Am Scheideweg: Christliche Motive in der
zeitgenössischen Kunst*, Kunsthalle Villa Kobe, Halle/Saale (G)
Marilyn Monroe - Life of a Legend, County Hall Gallery, London (G), Katalog

2002   *Objekte der Begierde*, Galerie Levy, Hamburg (G)
Olevano, Agentur für Zeitgenössische Kunst, Christoph Grau, Hamburg (E)
Schichtwechsel, Galerie Bebensee, Foto-Triennale-Hamburg, (G) Katalog
Stipendiaten Olevano, Museo-Centro Olevano Romano, Italien (G)
Images, l'Institute d'art, Marseille (G)
Reflected Images 2, Kunsthaus Hamburg, Hamburg (G), Katalog

2001   *Painterly Photography*, Blains Fine Art, London (G)
Marc Lüders-Photopicturen, Kunsthalle Hamburg, Hamburg (E), Katalog
Reflected Images, Kunsthalle Bern, Bern (G), Katalog
Palais für aktuelle Kunst, Glücksstadt (G)

2000   *Marc Lüders*, Kunstraum Carmen Oberst, Hamburg (E)

      Reflected Images - Das Bild in der Fotografie, Kunsthaus Hamburg, Hamburg (G)

      Alles 20% teurer, Galerie Andreas Schlüter, Hamburg (G)

1999   *Lifeproduktion,* Kampnagel KX, Hamburg (G)

      Forum für junge Kunst, Vereins- und Westbank, Hamburg (E), Katalog

      Badezimmer, Galerie Andreas Schlüter, Hamburg (E)

      Marc Lüders, Galerie 7/8 Barmherzigkeit, Hamburg (E)

      trans, Kunsthaus Hamburg, Hamburg (G)

      StipendiaTEN, Kunsthaus Hamburg, Hamburg (G)

1998   *Marc Lüders*, Kunstraum Clemens-Schultzstraße, Karen Koltermann, Hamburg, (E)

      Stipendiaten 97, Kunsthaus Hamburg, Hamburg (G), Katalog

E   = Einzelausstellung

G   = Gruppenausstellung

Selected Exhibitions

2008   *East Side Gallery*, Galerie Levy, Hamburg and pablo's birthday,
New York (S), Catalogue

2007   *Displaced Persons*, pablo's birthday, New York (S)

      Marc Lüders - Photopicturen, House of Art, Brno (S)

      Zwischen Konstruktion und Reduktion, Sammlung Hupertz, Stiftung Schleswig-
Holsteinische Landesmuseen Schloß Gottorf, Schleswig (G), Catalogue

      SCHÖNWAHNSINNIG, Sammlung CC, Stiftung Schleswig-Holsteinische
Landesmuseen Schloss Gottorf, Schleswig (G), Catalogue

2006   *In Flagranti II*, Dortmunder Kunstverein (G), Catalogue

      Vier Positionen zum Thema Landschaft, Galerie Kamolz, Braunschweig (G)

      Four German Artists, Sara Tecchia Gallery, New York (G)

2005   *Marc Lüders*, Artgalerie7, Köln (S)

      Painting on Photography - Photography on Painting, Museum of Contemporary
Photography, Chicago (G)

Marc Lüders, Wilhem-Hack-Museum, Rudolf-Scharpf-Galerie, Ludwigshafen (S)

Marc Lüders - Neue Photopicturen, Galerie Levy, Hamburg (S)

Marc Lüders, pablo's birthday, New York (S)

2004   *Marc Lüders*, Galerie Terminus, München (S)

Marc Lüders – Bildrealitäten, NORD/LB art gallery, Hannover (S), Catalogue

Der Mediale Blick des Malers II »Marc Lüders – Photopicturen«,
Galerie im Park, Bremen (S)

2003   *Marc Lüders - Photopicturen*, Galerie Levy, Hamburg (S), Catalogue

Der Augenblick ist Ewigkeit – Am Scheideweg: Christliche Motive in der
zeitgenössischen Kunst, Kunsthalle Villa Kobe, Halle/Saale (G)

Marilyn Monroe - Life of a Legend, County Hall Gallery, London (G), Catalogue

2002   *Objekte der Begierde*, Galerie Levy, Hamburg (G)

Olevano, Agentur für Zeitgenössische Kunst, Christoph Grau, Hamburg (S)

Schichtwechsel, Galerie Bebensee, Foto-Triennale-Hamburg (G), Catalogue

Images, l'Institute d'art, Marseille (G)

Reflected Images 2, Kunsthaus Hamburg, Hamburg (G), Catalogue

2001   *Painterly Photography*, Blains Fine Art, London (G)

Marc Lüders - Photopicturen, Kunsthalle Hamburg, Hamburg (S), Catalogue

Reflected Images, Kunsthalle Bern, Bern (G), Catalogue

2000   *Marc Lüders*, Kunstraum Carmen Oberst, Hamburg (S)

Reflected Images - Das Bild in der Fotografie, Kunsthaus Hamburg, Hamburg (G)

Alles 20 % teurer, Galerie Andreas Schlüter, Hamburg (G)

1999   *Lifeproduktion*, Kampnagel KX Hamburg (G)

Forum für junge Kunst, Vereins- und Westbank, Hamburg (S), Catalogue

Badezimmer, Galerie Andreas Schlüter, Hamburg (G)

Marc Lüders, Galerie 7/8 Barmherzigkeit, Hamburg (S)

trans, Kunsthaus , Hamburg (G)

StipendiaTEN, Kunsthaus Hamburg, Hamburg (G)

1998   *Marc Lüders*, Kunstraum Clemens-Schultzstraße, Karen Kollermann, Hamburg, (S)

Stipendiaten 97, Kunsthaus Hamburg, Hamburg (G), Catalogue

S   = Solo Exhibition

G   = Group Exhibition

Impressum / Colophon

Der Katalog erscheint anlässlich der Ausstellung / Catalogue to accompany the exhibition

MARC LÜDERS - EAST SIDE GALLERY
April - Mai 2008 / April - May 2008
Galerie Levy, Hamburg / pablo's birthday gallery, New York

Herausgegeben von / Edited by:
Galerie Levy, Hamburg / pablo's birthday gallery, New York
Texte / Essay: Jane Ursula Harris, New York / Ludwig Seyfarth, Berlin
Übersetzungen / Translations: Gillian Morris, Berlin / Andreas Münzner, Hamburg
Redaktion / Editing: Alexander Sairally, Hamburg
Gestaltung / Design: b3k-design, Claas Möller, Hamburg
Umschlagabbildung / Cover illustration: Marc Lüders, Vorderseite / front: *Figur 734-8-1*
Rückseite / back: *Figur 735-11-1*

Verlag und Druck / Printed and published by:
Kerber Verlag, Bielefeld
Windelbleicher Strasse 166 – 170
D-33659 Bielefeld
Germany
Tel. +49 (0) 5 21/9 50 08 10
Fax +49 (0) 5 21/9 50 08 88
e-mail: info@kerber-verlag.com
www.kerberverlag.de

US Distribution
D.A.P., Distributed Art Publishers Inc.
155 Sixth Avenue 2nd Floor
New York, N.Y. 10013
Tel. 001 212 6 27 19 99
Fax 001 212 6 27 94 84

ISBN 978-3-86678-159-7

Printed in Germany

Eine Collector's Edition mit einer signierten und nummerierten Photopictur (Ölfarbe auf Kodak Endura Metallic Print)
des Künstlers ist in einer Auflage von 18 Exemplaren und 5 Künstlerexemplaren erschienen und unter der ISBN 978-3-86678-160-3
beim Kerber Verlag erhältlich.

A Collector's Edition which includes a signed and numbered Photopictur (oil on Kodak Endura Metallic Print) by the artist was
published as a limited edition of 18 copies and 5 artist proofs. It is available at the publishing house, ISBN 978-3-86678-160-3.